THE HEALTHY MAKE-AHEAD COOKBOOK

the HEALTHY MAKE-AHEAD cookbook

Wholesome, Flavorful Freezer Meals
the Whole Family Will Enjoy

ROBIN DONOVAN

**ROCKRIDGE
PRESS**

For Doug and Cashel

CONTENTS

INTRODUCTION

IDEALLY, MEALTIMES ARE about more than just filling your belly. They're about savoring delicious, wholesome food and taking time to refuel, refresh, and revitalize while providing your body with the nutrition it needs to accomplish all the tasks you ask of it. Often, meals are also about connecting with family, friends, and loved ones. And most importantly, mealtimes should be enjoyable.

It's easy to agree with all the goals above, but considering the busy lives we lead, making healthy meals a reality day in and day out can be challenging. Between work, commutes, school drop-offs and pickups, errands, grocery shopping, and everything else you have to do every day, it's a wonder you manage to keep yourself and your family from starving to death!

If you're anything like me, the sirens of fast food, takeout, canned soups, and ready-to-eat meals from the supermarket are a constant distraction, luring you with their enticing song. Although you know these ultimately won't provide you with the healthy, homemade meals you want and need, you fight a daily inner battle: pick up something quick and nutritionally suspect, or completely stress yourself out trying to whip up a proper meal at the end of a long day. Happily, there is a solution, and you already have everything you need to make it a reality.

But let's back up a bit. I grew up eating nightly meals with my family. Times must have been simpler then, because somehow my mother always managed to get a freshly cooked meal on the table. Not only that, she also kept our kitchen stocked with quick-fix healthy options for breakfast, tasty and nutritious snacks, and plenty of great items to pack for a take-along school lunch.

During my first year of college, I lived in the dorms where the cafeteria opened three times a day, offering hot meals, an extensive salad bar, and all the cold cereal one could ever desire. Even if I missed a meal, a coffee shop just a few steps from my dorm room offered all sorts of snacks to get me through the day. The food wasn't the best, but it did the job.

Then, in my second year of college, I moved off campus and everything changed. I suddenly had to fend for myself, and I quickly developed a fondness for frozen chicken pot pies, frozen turkey tamales, canned tomato soup with grilled cheese sandwiches, and the fast-food drive-through. I missed my mom's cooking and even the dorm cafeteria. Most of all, I fantasized about having a freezer full of food that could be ready at a moment's notice. At that time, I wasn't overly concerned with issues like nutritional value, sodium levels, or calorie counts, but it did occur to me what a bonus it would be if those meals were healthy, too. However, I continued living fast and loose with my questionable store-bought and takeout meals.

Fast forward to a decade ago when I was very pregnant, and started to panic. "How am I going to feed myself when I'm home alone with a tiny baby?" I wondered. When I hit the eight-month mark in my pregnancy, I embarked on a frantic mission to fill my freezer with meals I could eat with one hand while holding an infant with the other. My baby came early, so I didn't quite manage the stockpile I was going for, but I'm convinced that those homemade frozen burritos and savory hand pies were instrumental to surviving the first few months of motherhood. I've been a devoted freezer-stocker ever since.

It turns out that a well-stocked freezer is incredibly useful, even for those without small children. These days, I no longer eat all my meals one-handed or cook with a sleeping infant strapped to my chest, but I still rarely have enough time to work, shop for ingredients, and prepare meals—let alone enjoy them—all on the same day. Now I plan ahead and spend a leisurely day in the kitchen, loading up the freezer with enough meals to handle any dining emergency that might arise in coming months.

My family and I are committed to eating nutrient-rich whole foods, so I've worked around the fact that many common make-ahead freezer recipes are loaded with cheese, pasta, and processed ingredients like canned cream of mushroom soup, or are heavy on sugar, sodium, and other unwanted additives. Even worse, many of these supposed time-saving recipes actually

take hours to prepare. As some critics have noted, those recipes don't save time, they just rearrange it.

This book will help demystify the process of stocking your freezer with make-ahead meals. With 125 dishes to choose from, you'll find you really can save time, make meals more enjoyable, and eat healthier. By devoting just a few hours to cooking on a Sunday, you'll create delicious meals to feed your family for weeks to come!

chapter one

MAKE-AHEAD BASICS

I love to cook, but when I finally get home at the end of a busy day, the dilemma of what to make for dinner can easily turn the joy of cooking into despair. So what's the solution? A stash of ready-to-go meals requiring minimal last-minute prep. This helps me reduce stress, limit unhealthy binges on fast food, and save money. Whether you simply cook a double batch of a recipe and stash half in the freezer for another time, or spend a Sunday making large batches of soups, stews, sauces, and more, building up your freezer supply will give you peace of mind (and a full and happy belly!) when you just have no time or energy for cooking.

THE MOST UNDERRATED APPLIANCE

Food processors and stand mixers get all the glory, but we've all got an amazing, futuristic, and incredibly useful appliance in our kitchen that rarely gets the credit it deserves: the freezer. In all its stoic silence, the freezer accepts whatever we place within it and keeps it fresh for months. The freezer works hard, to be sure, but it could do so much more if only we'd give it the chance. Thanks to this kitchen workhorse, many of your favorite meals—either fully cooked or prepped and frozen to be cooked later on—can be packed away, ready to feed you when hunger calls.

I like to freeze some dishes fully cooked so that all I have to do is reheat them, but others I like to freeze uncooked or as separate, mix-and-match components to be made fresh just before eating for maximum flavor and flexibility. In my freezer, you'll always find a variety, including heat-and-eat soups and stews, ready-to-cook meat loaves and burgers, cooked meatballs, multipurpose sauces, shredded cooked meat (chicken, pork, or beef), assembled but uncooked lasagnas and enchilada casseroles, cooked burritos and tamales, and assorted vegetables, both fully cooked and prepped but left uncooked.

Now if you assume my freezer is much more spacious than yours, I'm pretty sure you're wrong. I've got a very modest refrigerator with the freezer on top. But with a bit of organization, I manage to fill my unimpressive freezer with an impressive number of meals. And I have complete faith you can do the same with yours (okay, I'll admit, if you have a very large family, you might want to invest in a separate deep freezer).

HEALTHY MEETS MAKE-AHEAD

The case for make-ahead cooking is clear. It saves you time and reduces stress by helping you streamline your prepping and cooking, often allowing you to cook multiple meals at the same time. You will always have something healthy and delicious at the ready for dinner. And it saves you money and helps you meet dietary goals by allowing you to plan ahead, buy what you need (and take advantage of bulk prices), and use what you buy. Last but definitely not least, it helps you kick the processed food habit and eat more whole foods.

The recipes in this book rely on whole-food ingredients and limit the use of added sugar, processed and artificial ingredients, and ingredients high in saturated fats. You won't find creamy, cheesy, meaty casseroles, and pasta bakes. Rather, these dishes feature lots of vegetables, whole grains, and leaner meats, and they're more restrained with quantities of ingredients like cheese, cream, fatty meats, sodium, and sugar.

EQUIPMENT

Make-ahead meals don't require a lot of special equipment or supplies, but you'll need a few items on hand before you get started. The necessary cooking equipment really doesn't vary much from what you already have—a stove and oven, stockpot, saucepan, skillet, spoons and whisks, spatulas and tongs, and measuring cups and spoons.

Assuming you have a reasonably well-equipped kitchen, all you need before embarking on your make-ahead mission are supplies for storing and freezing your creations.

- **Heavy-duty plastic wrap and aluminum foil.** Aluminum foil is great for taking food from the freezer directly to the oven. Plastic wrap and foil both allow you to tightly wrap foods, protecting them from freezer burn.

- **Freezer-safe, resealable (zip-top) plastic bags in multiple sizes.** I primarily use quart and gallon sizes, but you may want smaller, pint-size bags for meal components and/or two-gallon bags for large cuts of meat. I use these to store most foods, from soups and stews to individual portions of meat or lasagna. The trick is to fill the bags, squeeze out any excess air, seal them tight, lay them flat on a sheet tray, and freeze until solid. Frozen flat in this way, they're easy to stack in the freezer.

- **Freezer-safe storage containers.** Plastic containers are lightweight and usually take up the least amount of room, but make sure yours are freezer safe and don't contain the chemical BPA, which can leach into food. I also like to use freezer containers that are both dishwasher and microwave safe. If you prefer to use glass instead of plastic, any option will do, including Pyrex containers and Mason jars. Having a variety of sizes available, from one to eight cups, is helpful. Note that square containers are more space efficient than round ones.

- **Permanent marker.** Labeling your meals clearly and completely is crucial. Believe me, I've proven this time and again: when "I'm sure I'll remember what that is" always becomes "What the . . . ?" Mark each packet or container with the name of the dish, thawing/reheating/serving instructions, and the date it was prepared. I also like to include the number of servings and any additional ingredients needed to finish the dish.

FIVE MONEY-SAVING TIPS

One of the great side benefits of make-ahead meals is their cost-effectiveness. Not only will you spend less on expensive takeout and prepared meals, you'll also be able to use your make-ahead routine to help you trim your budget in other ways.

1. **BUY IN-SEASON PRODUCE.** Fruits and vegetables are cheapest—and taste best—when they are in season. Buy extra, and prep and freeze for future meals.

2. **PLAN OUT YOUR MAKE-AHEAD COOKING AND MAKE A SHOPPING LIST.** At the store, stick to your list. Cutting out impulse buys will save you money and ensure that you don't end up with ingredients you don't know how to use.

3. **BUY THE LARGEST PACKAGE.** Buying food in greater quantities saves you money. Break large packages of meat, shredded cheese, and bread into recipe- or single-serving-size portions, and use them in make-ahead meals to stash in your freezer; you'll significantly reduce your price per portion.

4. **LOOK FOR SALES AND BUY IN BULK.** If whole chickens are on sale, buy a few and set aside a few hours to turn them into dozens of healthy meals.

5. **SKIP PREPARED SAUCES AND SALAD DRESSINGS.** Making your own from scratch costs much less than buying them bottled or jarred, and they usually taste better, too, as you can make them just the way you like.

- **Disposable aluminum baking pans in various sizes.** These come in all the same sizes as nondisposable baking pans and dishes—8 by 8 inches, 9 by 9 inches, 9 by 13 inches—and in various depths. They're excellent for storing dishes like lasagna or enchiladas, and they can go directly from the freezer to the oven. They also work for storing cakes and other baked foods.

- **Glass Mason jars with lids.** These are great for storing jams and jellies as well as sauces. They're microwavable and dishwasher safe, making them particularly convenient to use. Just be sure to always leave enough headspace to account for the expansion of liquid as it freezes.

- **Slow cooker.** You can certainly accomplish all of your make-ahead cooking without a slow cooker. However, if you have one, it will allow you to cook a meal while you're out of the house or multitask on a make-ahead cooking day; for example, you might cook a beef stew in the slow cooker while roasting a chicken in the oven and preparing soup on the stovetop, all at the same time.

- **Large stockpot.** A 6- or 8-quart stockpot is great for making large batches of soups and sauces.

- **Immersion blender.** These are handy for puréeing soups and sauces right in the pot, which saves time and makes a lot less mess than transferring to a blender or food processor.

- **Freezer thermometer.** You want to keep your freezer at 0°F or below, and a freezer thermometer lets you make sure you do.

- **Vacuum sealer.** Designed for make-ahead cooking, these handy machines suck the air out of your packaging, which protects food against freezer burn, helps maintain flavor, and maximizes storage space. Using a vacuum sealer to freeze solid foods is straightforward, but packing liquid foods is trickier. For highly liquid foods like soups and stews, it's best to freeze them first, remove them from the container in which they were frozen, and then vacuum seal the frozen food. This way you avoid both the machine inadvertently sucking out liquid along with the air (which makes a big mess) and the liquid expanding as it freezes (which compromises the seal).

MAKE-AHEAD METHODS

When you cook with make-ahead in mind, you don't have to drastically change your cooking techniques. Many of my make-ahead meals utilize the same methods I use for day-of cooking.

Below, you'll find some specific cooking techniques I employ in preparing make-ahead meals. All of them are easy, require the least possible cleanup, and produce delicious dishes.

SHEET PAN MEALS

Sheet pan meals can be entirely cooked on one large sheet pan. This type of cooking ticks all my boxes: it's easy, and it makes satisfying dishes with minimal mess. Sheet pan cooking is great for make-ahead meals, since you can cook multiple dishes on a single large pan, or even cook two pans full of food simultaneously.

ONE-POT MEALS

Like sheet pan meals, one-pot meals use just one pot (or baking dish) to cook all the elements of a meal—protein, veggies, and starch—providing ease of preparation and minimal cleanup. Soups, stews, chilies, and casseroles can all be made as delicious one-pot meals. These types of meals are also especially well suited to freezing for later.

SLOW COOKER

Perfect for cooking soups, stews, and braised meats, slow cookers allow you to prepare long-cooking dishes while you accomplish other tasks. A true set-and-forget gadget, the slow cooker frees you up to go about your life, or even cook other dishes on the stove or in the oven while a delicious make-ahead meal simmers away unattended.

PREP AND FREEZE

Prep-and-freeze meals are best frozen uncooked, then cooked just before eating. Meat and vegetable stir-fries, many egg-based dishes, and even some baked foods like pizzas and chicken tenders fall into this category. My recipes will lead you through prepping all the ingredients and then packing, freezing, thawing, cooking, and serving. Although these dishes require some last-minute cooking and assembly, all of the prep work is already done, so the cooking is quick and painless.

COOK AND STORE INDIVIDUAL PORTIONS

Many of the recipes here allow you to cook and/or store individual portions, so you can easily pull out one or several servings whenever you like. Methods vary; you'll use a different technique when cooking egg dishes, pasta bakes, or meat loaves in ramekins than when forming and wrapping individual pizzas, burger patties, or portions of meat.

WHAT TO AVOID

While most foods can be frozen successfully, a few do not freeze well. These include:

- **FRUITS WITH HIGH WATER CONTENTS** like apples, citrus fruits, and watermelon, which turn to mush when thawed.

- **VEGETABLES WITH HIGH WATER CONTENTS** like tomatoes, potatoes, lettuce, cucumbers, celery, and radishes. However, some of these, like potatoes, will freeze just fine if you cook them first.

- **MAYONNAISE** will separate and lose flavor quickly when frozen. Avoid freezing not only mayonnaise but also any foods containing it, like tuna or chicken salads, dips and spreads, or crab cakes.

- **CREAMY DAIRY PRODUCTS** including soft cheeses (Brie, Camembert), cottage cheese, sour cream, cream cheese, and yogurt. Also, blocks of cheese become crumbly when frozen, but shredded cheeses freeze well.

- **EGGS SHOULD NEVER BE FROZEN IN THEIR SHELLS**, because the liquid inside expands when frozen, leading to eggsplosions. On the other hand, you can freeze whole eggs, beaten eggs, or egg whites. Egg yolks can also be frozen, but add a bit of sugar or salt to them first to prevent them from turning to gel.

- **FRESH HERBS** lose their flavor when frozen by themselves. Instead, mince the herbs and freeze them with olive oil in an ice cube tray.

THE ART OF STORAGE

Successful make-ahead cooking requires finesse in food storage. If you've got a separate upright or chest freezer, your only concern will be remembering to label and organize your foods for easy access. If you're like me and have only a fridge-top freezer compartment, storage becomes a bit trickier, but rest assured, you can store quite a few ready-made meals even in a small freezer.

ORGANIZATION IS YOUR FRIEND

This begins with devising your meal plan and shopping lists, and continues right through cooking, storing, and serving your make-ahead meals. Start with a well-thought-out plan that includes not just what you'll cook but also how and where you'll store those meals. Before you start cooking, consider the following questions:

- Will you store the food in one large container, in small or large resealable plastic bags, wrapped in plastic wrap or foil, or in individual storage containers?

- How much and what type of storage space do you have available?

- How and when do you intend to serve the food?

LABEL SMART

It's helpful to know not only what's in each container, but also when it was made, the number of servings it contains, and how to reheat and serve its contents. All this can be written either directly on storage containers (if using single-use containers like plastic bags) or on food labels that can be removed or labeled over later. My labeling format looks like this:

NAME OF DISH

QUANTITY

DATE COOKED/PACKED

REHEATING/SERVING INSTRUCTIONS

FREEZER TIPS

Filling your freezer with finesse is an art. Here are a few tips and tricks to help you get the most out of your freezer.

- **Keep your freezer sufficiently cold.** To safely freeze foods, the temperature of your freezer must remain at or below 0°F. If you're unsure of your freezer's temperature, invest in an inexpensive freezer thermometer.

- **Store foods in categories** such as raw meat, cooked meals, fruit, vegetables, etc., and use plastic bins to separate foods. I like to use these bins to store foods by type, such as fruits, veggies, raw meat, or individual prepared foods like burritos and mini pizzas.

- **Use ice cube trays** to freeze small, measured portions of ingredients like lemon juice, tomato paste, pesto, or leftover bacon grease. Pop the frozen cubes out of the tray and store them in labeled plastic bags, or vacuum seal the cubes in plastic. You can toss frozen cubes directly into a hot pan or pot, or thaw them to add to unheated foods.

- **Freeze foods flat in plastic bags,** then "file" them in labeled boxes or bins for easy retrieval.

- **Be mindful of foods you shouldn't freeze,** like food in cans and whole eggs in the shell.

The water inside will expand when frozen, causing the shell or container to crack open and explode. Soft cheeses, yogurt, mayonnaise, white potatoes, and cooked eggs are perfectly safe to freeze but their texture will suffer when frozen.

- **Achieve a vacuum-sealed effect** with many frozen foods—even without a vacuum sealer. When freezing food in plastic bags, seal the bag most of the way, then insert a straw into the small opening left. Suck any remaining air out of the bag, quickly remove the straw, and seal the bag the rest of the way.

MEAL PLANNING

Without a plan, the idea of preparing 30 meals may be overwhelming. Even if you manage to fill your freezer, you may not end up with a variety of foods that keep you and your family satisfied for any period of time. In the following chapter, I provide meal plans for groups of dishes to store together in your freezer, whether you're anticipating big life events or just busy everyday living. I also teach you how to cook all these make-ahead meals in one go. (It's less daunting than you think.)

As I said before, a good plan can save you time and money, lower your stress, and help you and your family enjoy nutritious meals every day.

- **Take an inventory of the ingredients you currently have.** Using these as a starting point will help you make the most of what you've already purchased and make space for storing your prepared meals.

- **Choose recipes based on ingredients** in your kitchen, what is on sale at the supermarket (check store sale ads), and the kinds of foods your family enjoys eating.

- **Once you've decided which meals to cook and in what quantities, create a detailed shopping list.** Go through each recipe and write down the ingredients you'll need to purchase. If you're using the same ingredient in more than one recipe, keep track of the total quantity with tally marks.

- **Group items on your shopping list according to category—produce, meat, spices, baking items, etc.** Making your list on your computer, phone, or tablet will simplify sorting and arranging once all the items have been added.

- **Think through packaging and storage.** Decide how you will package the foods and make sure you have the necessary supplies, like bags, containers, wraps, and labeling supplies. Add any missing items to your list.

- **Create a cooking plan.** Determine the order to cook the meals, create a prep list for the ingredients, and estimate how much time you need to get it all done. In the next chapter, I'll detail how to streamline your prep.

- **Do your shopping.** Head out to the market (or markets), and purchase all the ingredients and supplies on your list.

- **Go time!** Start with prep, then move on to cooking, following your plan. Once the meals have finished cooking, let them cool to room temperature.

- **Pack up your meals, label them, and refrigerate until cold.** Transfer to the freezer.

- **Keep a running freezer inventory** so you'll always know what meals you have available.

THAWING FOODS SAFELY

There are three ways to safely thaw food: in the refrigerator overnight, submerged in a bowl of cold water, or in the microwave. Some foods can be cooked directly from a frozen state without thawing at all. Every recipe in this book includes detailed thawing, reheating, and serving instructions, but below are some helpful guidelines.

THAWING MEAT, POULTRY, FISH, AND SEAFOOD

The safest way to defrost raw meat, poultry, fish, and seafood is to thaw it in the refrigerator. Simply place the packages of frozen food on a sheet pan or in a baking dish, then refrigerate overnight until completely thawed.

If you don't have time for refrigerator thawing, submerge the raw meat or fish, tightly sealed in a plastic bag, in a bowl of cold water, changing the water every 30 minutes. With this method, the food will defrost in anywhere from 30 minutes to several hours, depending on the size of the package.

If necessary, frozen foods can be thawed in the microwave. Remove any packaging, place the food in a microwave-safe dish, and thaw according to the microwave manufacturer's instructions. Note that food thawed in a microwave must be fully cooked immediately after thawing.

THAWING PREPARED DISHES

Some prepared dishes, like pasta bakes, casseroles, enchiladas, and frittatas, are best fully defrosted before cooking or reheating. For optimum results, place the frozen items (still wrapped or packed in freezer containers) on a baking sheet and thaw in the refrigerator overnight.

Other prepared foods, especially baked foods like pizzas or pies, can be baked straight out of the freezer. Burritos, soups, stews, chilies, and many other fully cooked foods can be reheated in either the microwave or the oven, or on the stovetop directly from a frozen state.

To help remove frozen soups or stews from their plastic bags, place them in a bowl of hot water for about five minutes, just until the contents soften enough for you to break them up and transfer them to a pot or bowl for reheating.

THAWING VEGETABLES AND FRUITS

Most raw vegetables can be cooked without defrosting. Add them directly to soups, stews, chilies, or stir-fries toward the end of cooking, or add them directly to egg mixtures for quiche or frittatas. You can also steam raw, frozen vegetables in either a stovetop steamer or a covered dish in a microwave with a bit of water.

Fruit can be used in numerous recipes without thawing first. Add frozen berries or chunks of frozen peach, pineapple, mango, or banana directly to pancakes, cake, or bread batter. For a quick, cold smoothie, add frozen fruit to a blender along with a bit of milk or milk substitute.

WHAT NOT TO DO

Never thaw raw foods on the countertop or at room temperature. Harmful germs can multiply quickly at room temperature, making the food unsafe to eat.

Never thaw foods in hot water. As at room temperature, harmful germs can multiply quickly as the thawed portions of the food warm up from contact with the hot water.

Never cook frozen meat in a slow cooker—the warm temperature can encourage the growth of harmful bacteria.

8 HEALTHY FREEZER HACKS

Your freezer doesn't just save you time and money; it can help you eat healthier, too. Here are my eight favorite healthy freezer hacks.

1. SAVE ODDS AND ENDS—bones, vegetable trimmings, and so on—to make nourishing stock or broth to be used in your recipes. Store homemade stock in quart-size plastic bags in your freezer.

2. PREP AND MEASURE INGREDIENTS FOR STIR-FRIES, then package them together so they're ready to use for a quick, easy, healthy meal at a moment's notice. Combine stir-fry vegetables in one plastic bag, aromatics like chopped ginger and garlic in another, and protein in a third. Store all three together in one gallon-size, zip-top plastic bag.

3. BUY DARK, LEAFY GREENS LIKE CHARD, KALE, OR SPINACH IN BULK. Wash, dry, and chop the greens. Let them dry completely and freeze in resealable plastic bags in recipe-size portions.

4. FREEZE FRESH HERBS IN AN ICE CUBE TRAY with a bit of olive oil.

5. COOK LARGE BATCHES OF DRIED BEANS that can be frozen and used in chilies, veggie burgers, burritos, soups, or salads.

6. MAKE INSTANT BANANA "ICE CREAM" by freezing peeled and diced bananas, then whirling them in a blender or food processor until smooth. You can dress it up by adding peanut or almond butter, or chocolate syrup or chips.

7. COOK LARGE BATCHES OF BROWN RICE and other long-cooking whole grains, then freeze them in individual portions that are easy to heat and serve.

8. FREEZE TRIMMED AND DICED IN-SEASON FRUIT—especially peaches, nectarines, apricots, cherries, berries, mango, and pineapple—on a large baking sheet, then transfer to a resealable plastic bag for the makings of healthy smoothies all year long. (You can even add some of those frozen greens you stashed!) Or up the ante and store combinations of fruit in individual bags, then just empty a bag into the blender, add your liquid of choice and any other add-ins, and blend for a quick meal.

ABOUT THE RECIPES

From satisfying breakfasts to celebration-worthy desserts, all recipes here are prepared with fresh, whole ingredients available at your local grocery store.

We begin with wholesome breakfasts both sweet and savory, like Toasted Oat, Nut, and Honey Breakfast Bars and Egg-and-Cheese Mini Breakfast Tostada Cups. For midday and dinner meals, Chicken and Sausage Gumbo and Spicy Beef-and-Bean Chili will appeal to the meat eaters, while vegetarian mains include hearty meals like Black Bean and Roasted Chile Burritos and Creamy Mac and Cheese with Broccoli and Silken Tofu. The fish and seafood recipes are diverse and delicious, featuring dishes like Spicy Orange Broccoli-Shrimp Stir-Fry and Fish Tacos with Pineapple Salsa.

For snacks, consider the Fruit-and-Nut Frozen Yogurt Bites and Whole-Wheat Pizza Pinwheels; side dishes round out your meals, such as Rich Baked Beans with Bacon and Molasses and Quinoa Pilaf with Dried Apricots and Almonds.

Of course, I've included several delectable desserts, starting on page 169.

Perhaps most importantly, I provide strategies for planning, shopping, prepping, cooking, storing, and freezing, including instructions for serving and reheating, so you can choose to eat the dishes straightaway or save them for another time.

Recipe labels are included on each recipe for your dietary needs, including paleo, gluten-free, vegan, and vegetarian. Some recipes include tips for adjusting recipes. Don't forget—vegan recipes are vegetarian, too!

FREEZER PARTY

There's no need to cook make-ahead meals alone. Have a freezer party with friends and knock out enough meals to stock all of your freezers. It's cost effective, efficient, and best of all, fun! Here's a step-by-step guide to throwing your own enjoyable and productive freezer party.

Invite Your Friends

Limit your group to four to six people total. When choosing who to invite, consider dietary restrictions (you don't want one vegetarian thrown in with five meat eaters), and those with similar needs (people with/without kids, for instance).

Choose a Location and a Date

Choose the house with the best kitchen for cooking and set the date.

Create a Menu

Ask the group to suggest recipes that are fairly simple, scalable, and good for freezing. Stress that the recipes should be ones they've successfully made before.

Consider cooking methods when choosing your menu. For example, don't take on several recipes that need to roast in the oven before freezing.

Choose four to six recipes, no more than one recipe per participant. (If you have four people, choose a maximum of four recipes.) Double, triple, or quadruple the recipes as needed, so you end up with enough for each person to take home at least eight servings. For instance, if you have four participants and you make four dishes that each produce eight servings, each person can take home two servings of each recipe. Start small for your first party, but feel free to tackle more as you become more experienced.

Print out each recipe with instructions up to and including freezing. These should also include thawing, cooking, and reheating instructions. Make enough copies of each recipe for each participant to have one.

Do Your Shopping

Make one master shopping list for the ingredients and packing supplies (disposable baking pans, plastic wrap, resealable freezer bags, etc.) for all the recipes. Assign one person to do all of the shopping, or have a couple people to do it together. Save receipts and split the cost.

Do an Equipment Check

Check the kitchen where the party will take place to make sure all the necessary cooking equipment (food processors, blenders, knives, pots and pans, etc.) is available. If anything is missing, ask people to bring whatever items are needed.

Gather labeling supplies—stickers, Sharpies, and anything else you'll need to label the packages of food that people will take home.

Get Ready

Make sure the kitchen is clean and tidy, and that there is ample freezer and refrigerator space available for all.

Provide a station for each participant with a cutting board, knife, dishtowel, and any other necessary equipment.

Start Cooking

When everyone arrives, divvy up the recipes, placing one person in charge of each. If multiple dishes require the same prep (such as dicing onions or slicing a pork shoulder into two-inch pieces), have one person do it all and then set the prepped ingredients aside for the group.

Discuss the order in which cooking will be carried out so everyone has the time they need at the stove.

Prep the dishes. Let everything cool to room temperature before packing. Pack the food up in individual servings, and clearly label each package with the name of the dish; number of servings in the package; and thawing, reheating, and serving instructions.

Clean Up

Don't stick the host with all the cleanup! Leave the kitchen as clean as you found it.

chapter two

MEAL PLANS

Make-ahead meals are particularly helpful when planning for big events like the birth of a baby, or busy times like back-to-school season or the holidays. To be sure you prepare enough food to get you through those potentially stressful times, it's a good idea to have an organized strategy. This chapter provides five of my favorite meal plans to see you through various life events.

Cocoa-Banana Baked Oatmeal Cups • Ready-to-Cook Ham, Cheddar, and Green Chile Quiche • Spicy Beef-and-Bean Chili • Vegan Black Bean Veggie Burgers • Smoked Turkey and Pesto Panini with Sun-Dried Tomatoes • Coconut-Almond Energy Bites with Chocolate Chips

If you have school-age kids, the start of school in fall is always hectic. The whole family is adjusting to a new, tighter schedule, usually with less time to get out the door in the morning. And of course, kids (and parents!) need a good breakfast to start the day right. This plan includes five dishes for breakfast, lunch, and dinner that will serve an average family of four or five, plus a snack or treat making 36 pieces. A couple of these make extra portions, but you can always stash them for future meals. All can be cooked and packed for freezing in under two hours.

PREP

Start with the **Spicy Beef-and-Bean Chili**. Heat the oil in a Dutch oven, and sauté the onions and garlic. Brown the beef and then add the remaining ingredients. Bring to a boil and then let simmer for one hour. Cool to room temperature. *[Spicy Beef and Bean Chili is ready for packing.]*

While the chili simmers, preheat the oven to 350°F, and lightly oil a muffin tin for the **Cocoa-Banana Baked Oatmeal Cups**. Mix together the ingredients, and spoon them into the muffin tin. Bake in the preheated oven for 30 minutes. Cool to room temperature. *[Cocoa-Banana Baked Oatmeal Cups are ready for packing.]*

While waiting for the pancakes and other foods to cool, mix up the egg mixture for the **Ready-to-Cook Ham, Cheddar, and Green Chile Quiche**. Put the mixture into a labeled, resealable plastic bag, and freeze as directed in the recipe. *[Ready-to-Cook Ham, Cheddar, and Green Chile Quiche is done.]*

Mix and form the **Vegan Black Bean Veggie Burgers**. Wrap the burgers individually in plastic wrap, or cut squares of parchment to separate the burgers to prevent sticking. *[Vegan Black Bean Veggie Burgers are done.]*

Assemble the **Smoked Turkey and Pesto Panini with Sun-Dried Tomatoes**. Wrap each sandwich individually in plastic wrap, and freeze as directed in the recipe. *[Smoked Turkey and Pesto Panini with Sun-Dried Tomatoes are done.]*

Mix and freeze the **Coconut-Almond Energy Bites with Chocolate Chips** as directed in the recipe. *[Coconut-Almond Energy Bites with Chocolate Chips are done.]*

Once the chili and oatmeal cups have cooled to room temperature, pack and freeze them according to the instructions in the recipes. *[Spicy Beef-and-Bean Chili and Cocoa-Banana Baked Oatmeal Cups are done.]*

RECIPES

COCOA-BANANA BAKED OATMEAL CUPS

PAGE 39	SERVES 12	PREP 10 MINS	
			FREEZE: Wrap each baked oatmeal cup tightly in plastic wrap, and freeze together in a large, resealable plastic bag.
			THAW: Heat from frozen in the microwave on high for about two minutes.

READY-TO-COOK HAM, CHEDDAR, AND GREEN CHILE QUICHE

PAGE 47	SERVES 8	PREP 10 MINS	
			FREEZE: Freeze the egg mixture flat in a large, resealable plastic bag.
			THAW: Thaw in the refrigerator for 24 hours, and then bake, in either a pie crust or a pie dish without crust, for 40 to 50 minutes.

SPICY BEEF-AND-BEAN CHILI

PAGE 64	SERVES 8 TO 10	PREP 10 MINS	
			FREEZE: Freeze in individual-serving-size containers, or in one gallon-size or two quart-size resealable plastic bags.
			THAW: Thaw in the refrigerator overnight, in the microwave, or on the stove-top. Reheat on the stovetop or in the microwave.

VEGAN BLACK BEAN VEGGIE BURGERS

PAGE 72	SERVES 4	PREP 10 MINS	
			FREEZE: Freeze the burgers individually wrapped or with squares of parchment separating them in a large, resealable plastic bag.
			THAW: Cook from frozen in a bit of cooking oil in a hot skillet for about 7 minutes per side. Serve hot on hamburger buns with mustard, ketchup, onions, lettuce, or your preferred burger toppings.

SMOKED TURKEY AND PESTO PANINI WITH SUN-DRIED TOMATOES

PAGE 111	SERVES 4	PREP 5 MINS	
			FREEZE: Freeze the wrapped sandwiches in a large, resealable plastic bag.
			THAW: Cook from frozen in olive oil or butter in a skillet for 4 to 5 minutes per side.

COCONUT-ALMOND ENERGY BITES WITH CHOCOLATE CHIPS

PAGE 141	SERVES 36	PREP 15 MINS	
			FREEZE: Freeze balls on a baking sheet, then transfer to a large, resealable plastic bag.
			THAW: Thaw at room temperature for 30 minutes or in the microwave for 20 to 30 seconds.

Gluten-Free Blueberry Pancake Muffins • Sweet Potato Hash and Eggs • Black Bean and Roasted Chile Burritos • Whole-Wheat Pasta Bake with Mushrooms and Radicchio • Inside-Out Cheeseburgers • Honey-Nut Snack Squares

Do yourself or any pregnant loved one a favor. Load the freezer with these five dishes (8 to 12 servings), plus a sweet treat that makes 16 pieces. All of these are easy to thaw and reheat—and possible to eat with one hand while holding a baby with the other. (The brand-new parent will thank their lucky stars, too.) All this can be whipped up in less than two hours.

PREP

Start with the **Sweet Potato Hash and Eggs**. Preheat the oven to 425°F. Prep the vegetables and bake them on a large baking sheet for 30 to 40 minutes.

Meanwhile, boil a pot of water for the **Whole-Wheat Pasta Bake with Mushrooms and Radicchio**.

While waiting, scramble the eggs for the hash until just set, then transfer them to a plate and let cool to room temperature. Shred the cheese and chop the scallions. When the vegetables are roasted, remove them from the oven and let them cool to room temperature. Reduce the oven heat to 400°F.

Add the pasta to the boiling water. Then prep the vegetables and sauté the mushrooms. Drain the pasta, combine it with all the other ingredients, and transfer to a 9-by-13-inch baking dish. Bake for 30 minutes and let cool to room temperature. Reduce the oven to 350°F.

While the pasta bakes, pack and freeze the Sweet Potato Hash and Eggs. *[Sweet Potato Hash and Eggs done.]*

Next, prep the muffin tin for the **Gluten-Free Blueberry Pancake Muffins**. Mix the batter and fill the muffin cups. Bake for 15 to 18 minutes, then let cool to room temperature.

While the muffins bake, assemble the **Black Bean and Roasted Chile Burritos**. Pack and freeze. *[Black Bean and Roasted Chile Burritos are done.]*

Pack and freeze the Whole-Wheat Pasta Bake with Mushrooms and Radicchio. *[Whole-Wheat Pasta Bake with Mushrooms and Radicchio is done.]*

Wrap the cooled Gluten-Free Blueberry Pancake Muffins individually and freeze. *[Gluten-Free Blueberry Pancake Muffins are done.]*

Line an 8-by-8-inch baking pan with parchment paper, and mix the ingredients for the **Honey-Nut Snack Squares**. Press the mixture into the pan, and bake for 20 minutes. Remove from the oven and cool on a wire rack.

Meanwhile, prepare the mixture for the **Inside-Out Cheeseburgers** and form the patties. Wrap and freeze. *[Inside-Out Cheeseburgers are done.]*

When the Honey-Nut Snack Squares are cool, lift them from the pan using the parchment paper, then cut, wrap, and freeze. *[Honey-Nut Snack Squares are done.]*

GLUTEN-FREE BLUEBERRY PANCAKE MUFFINS

PAGE 42	SERVES 12	PREP 5 MINS	**FREEZE:** Wrap the muffins individually in plastic wrap and freeze.
			THAW: Reheat from frozen on a microwave-safe plate in the microwave for about 2 minutes, or wrapped in foil in a 350°F oven for 10 to 15 minutes.

SWEET POTATO HASH AND EGGS

PAGE 45	SERVES 12	PREP 15 MINS	**FREEZE:** Assemble the bowls in individual-size, microwave-safe storage containers, and freeze.
			THAW: Reheat from frozen in the microwave on 50 percent power, stirring every 30 seconds or so, until heated through.

BLACK BEAN AND ROASTED CHILE BURRITOS

PAGE 70	SERVES 12	PREP 20 MINS	**FREEZE:** Wrap the burritos individually in plastic wrap and freeze.
			THAW: Wrap in a damp paper towel, then thaw in the microwave for about 4 minutes, turning once.

WHOLE-WHEAT PASTA BAKE WITH MUSHROOMS AND RADICCHIO

PAGE 84	SERVES 8	PREP 10 MINS	**FREEZE:** Divide the pasta among individual-size, microwave-safe storage containers and freeze.
			THAW: Reheat from frozen in the microwave or covered with aluminum foil in a 400°F oven for about 40 minutes.

INSIDE-OUT CHEESEBURGERS

PAGE 127	SERVES 8	PREP 15 MINS	**FREEZE:** Wrap the burger patties individually and freeze.
			THAW: Thaw the burgers completely in the refrigerator overnight, and cook as directed in the recipe, or cook from frozen for 8 to 10 minutes per side. Serve on hamburger buns with traditional burger fixings.

HONEY-NUT SNACK SQUARES

PAGE 144	SERVES 16	PREP 10 MINS	**FREEZE:** Cut into 16 squares, wrap individually in plastic wrap, and freeze.
			THAW: Thaw at room temperature overnight.

Coconut Brown Rice Pudding • Whole-Grain Buttermilk Raspberry Muffins •
Soba Noodles and Tofu in Spicy Peanut Sauce • Fish Tacos with Pineapple Salsa •
Homemade Crunchy Chicken Tenders • Strawberry Frozen Yogurt Pops

Before summer hits, fill your freezer with these light, refreshing meals. Apart from the breakfast pudding and muffins, which make additional servings, these recipes all serve four to six people, and the entire meal plan can be produced in less than two hours. For larger families, simply double the recipes.

PREP

Start by preheating the oven to 400°F and combining the rice and water for the **Coconut Brown Rice Pudding** in a saucepan. Bring to a boil, then cover and simmer for 30 minutes.

While the rice is cooking, lightly oil a muffin tin for the **Whole-Grain Buttermilk Raspberry Muffins**. Mix the batter and transfer it to the muffin tin. Bake in the preheated oven for 15 to 20 minutes. Remove from the oven, and let muffins cool to room temperature on a wire rack. Pack and freeze. *[Whole-Grain Buttermilk Raspberry Muffins are done.]*

When the rice has finished simmering, reduce the heat to low, stir in the remaining ingredients, and continue to cook, covered, for 30 more minutes. Remove from the heat and let cool to room temperature. Pack and freeze. *[Coconut Brown Rice Pudding is done.]*

Boil a pot of water and cook the noodles for the **Soba Noodles and Tofu in Spicy Peanut Sauce**. While the noodles are cooking, combine the sauce ingredients, and prep the tofu and carrots. Once the noodles are cooked, drain and transfer to a large bowl. Add the sauce, tofu, and carrots, and toss to mix. Let cool to room temperature, pack, and freeze. *[Soba Noodles and Tofu in Spicy Peanut Sauce is done.]*

Start the **Strawberry Frozen Yogurt Pops** by combining the strawberries and sugar. Let sit for 15 minutes.

Meanwhile, make the spice mixture for the **Fish Tacos with Pineapple Salsa** and season the fish. Prep and mix the ingredients for the salsa. Pack and freeze. *[Fish Tacos with Pineapple Salsa are done.]*

Line a large, rimmed baking sheet with parchment paper, and prepare the flour mixture, egg mixture, and bread crumbs for the **Homemade Crunchy Chicken Tenders**. Coat the chicken pieces in the flour, egg, and crumbs, and arrange them in a single layer on the baking sheet. Freeze and pack. *[Homemade Crunchy Chicken Tenders are done.]*

Blend the macerated strawberries with the remaining ingredients for the Strawberry Frozen Yogurt Pops. Transfer to ice-pop molds and freeze. *[Strawberry Frozen Yogurt Pops are done.]*

COCONUT BROWN RICE PUDDING

PAGE 40	SERVES 10	PREP 5 MINS	
			FREEZE: Divide the yogurt into 10 cups of a lightly oiled muffin tin. Cover and freeze. Once frozen, pop the puddings out of the muffin tin, wrap individually in plastic wrap, and store in one large, resealable plastic bag.
			THAW: Thaw overnight in the refrigerator or microwave, and serve chilled or at room temperature.

WHOLE-GRAIN BUTTERMILK RASPBERRY MUFFINS

PAGE 43	SERVES 12	PREP 10 MINS	
			FREEZE: Wrap the muffins individually in plastic wrap and freeze.
			THAW: To serve, thaw muffins completely at room temperature, or reheat in the microwave or, wrapped in foil, in a 350°F oven.

SOBA NOODLES AND TOFU IN SPICY PEANUT SAUCE

PAGE 75	SERVES 4	PREP 15 MINS	
			FREEZE: Divide the sauced noodles into individual storage containers and freeze.
			THAW: Reheat from frozen in a skillet on the stovetop, adding a bit of water as needed, or in the microwave.

FISH TACOS WITH PINEAPPLE SALSA

PAGE 93	SERVES 4 TO 6	PREP 15 MINS	
			FREEZE: Wrap each seasoned fish fillet in plastic wrap and freeze. Freeze tortillas and salsa alongside in separate resealable plastic bags.
			THAW: Thaw in the refrigerator overnight. Cook the thawed fish in a skillet. Heat the tortillas, wrapped in foil, in the oven.

HOMEMADE CRUNCHY CHICKEN TENDERS

PAGE 107	SERVES 4	PREP 10 MINS	
			FREEZE: Freeze the coated chicken pieces on the baking sheet until frozen solid, at least 2 hours. Transfer the chicken tenders to a large, resealable plastic bag.
			THAW: To serve, cook from frozen in a 350°F oven on a parchment-lined baking sheet for 40 minutes.

STRAWBERRY FROZEN YOGURT POPS

PAGE 172	SERVES 6	PREP 5 MINS	
			FREEZE: Freeze in the ice-pop molds. Keep frozen until ready to serve.

Maple-Pecan Pumpkin Bread • Tuscan-Style White Bean and Kale Soup • Butternut Squash, Spinach, and Black Bean Enchiladas • Fennel and Tomato Baked Halibut Fillets • Slow-Cooked Short Ribs with Carrots and Mushrooms • Superfood Chocolate Bark

Diets can go off the rails during the holiday season. Stay on track: stock the freezer with white bean soup, vegetarian enchiladas, and a chocolate bark filled with superfoods. With this plan, you'll provide healthy options for yourself and your family (the recipes serve between 4 and 8), plus treats with extra for guests. For large numbers, simply double or even triple the recipes, if necessary. It can be made in under two hours.

PREP

Preheat the oven to 350°F and lightly oil a 9-by-5-inch loaf pan for the **Maple-Pecan Pumpkin Bread**. Mix the ingredients together, then transfer the batter to the prepared loaf pan. Bake in the preheated oven for 35 minutes.

Meanwhile, prepare the **Tuscan-Style White Bean and Kale Soup**, mashing the beans, sautéing the vegetables in the stockpot, and adding the remaining ingredients. Cover the soup and simmer for 20 minutes.

Remove the Maple-Pecan Pumpkin Bread from the oven. Raise the heat to 400°F. Let the bread cool in the pan for 10 minutes. Slice or remove from pan whole, and cool completely. Pack and freeze. *[Maple-Pecan Pumpkin Bread is done.]*

As the soup simmers, prep the squash for the **Butternut Squash, Spinach, and Black Bean Enchiladas**. Roast it in the oven for 20 minutes. Meanwhile, make the **Red Chile Sauce**.

When the soup is finished, remove it from the heat, and cool to room temperature. Pack and freeze. *[Tuscan-Style White Bean and Kale Soup done.]*

Prep the **Slow-Cooked Short Ribs with Carrots and Mushrooms**; season the meat and divide it and the vegetables between two gallon-size resealable plastic bags. Freeze. *[Slow-Cooked Short Ribs with Carrots and Mushrooms are done.]*

Make the tomato sauce for the **Fennel and Tomato Baked Halibut Fillets**. While it simmers, assemble the Butternut Squash, Spinach, and Black Bean Enchiladas in two 7-by-11-inch baking dishes, leaving off the cheese. Cover and freeze in resealable plastic bags (one portion for each pan of enchiladas, and a separate bag for the cheese). Cover tightly and freeze. *[Butternut Squash, Spinach, and Black Bean Enchiladas are done.]*

Make the **Superfood Chocolate Bark**. Cool and freeze. *[Superfood Chocolate Bark is done.]*

When the tomato sauce for the halibut is done, cool to room temperature.

Season the fish for the Fennel and Tomato Baked Halibut Fillets, and pack them into one or two resealable plastic bags. Pack the sauce separately into one or two large zip-top bags. Freeze the fish fillets and sauce together, with the sauce lying flat. *[Fennel and Tomato Baked Halibut Fillets are done.]*

MAPLE-PECAN PUMPKIN BREAD

PAGE 38	SERVES 12	PREP 10 MINS	**FREEZE:** Slice the loaf into 12 slices. Wrap each slice individually in plastic wrap or place squares of parchment between the slices and wrap the whole loaf tightly in plastic wrap. Freeze in a large, resealable plastic bag.
			THAW: To serve, thaw at room temperature for an hour or two, or toast lightly.

TUSCAN-STYLE WHITE BEAN AND KALE SOUP

PAGE 53	SERVES 8	PREP 10 MINS	**FREEZE:** Portion the soup into single-serving storage containers to freeze or transfer into one or two large, resealable plastic bags and freeze flat.
			THAW: Thaw in the refrigerator overnight or in the microwave, and reheat either on the stovetop or in the microwave.

BUTTERNUT SQUASH, SPINACH, AND BLACK BEAN ENCHILADAS

PAGE 73	SERVES 5	PREP 25 MINS	**FREEZE:** Cover the assembled, uncooked enchiladas (minus the cheese) tightly with aluminum foil or plastic wrap, and freeze. Place the shredded cheese in a resealable plastic bag and freeze.
			THAW: To serve, sprinkle the cheese over the top, and heat, covered with aluminum foil, in a 350°F oven for about 50 minutes, removing the foil for the last 15 minutes.

FENNEL AND TOMATO BAKED HALIBUT FILLETS

PAGE 94	SERVES 4 TO 6	PREP 10 MINS	**FREEZE:** Freeze the sauce flat in one or two large, resealable plastic bags. Wrap the seasoned fish fillets individually in plastic wrap, and freeze in a large, resealable plastic bag alongside the sauce.
			THAW: Thaw the fish and sauce overnight in the refrigerator or in a bowl of cold water (still sealed in their plastic bags) for up to an hour, changing the water once. Cook according to the recipe.

SLOW-COOKED SHORT RIBS WITH CARROTS AND MUSHROOMS

PAGE 136	SERVES 6	PREP 10 MINS	**FREEZE:** Freeze the meat and vegetables in two gallon-size, resealable plastic bags. Make a note on each bag that you'll need six cups of beef broth and one tablespoon of cornstarch to cook the dish.
			THAW: Thaw in the refrigerator for at least 24 hours, then transfer to the slow cooker, add the broth, and cook as directed in the recipe.

SUPERFOOD CHOCOLATE BARK

PAGE 183	MAKES 1 ¾ POUNDS	PREP 10 MINS	**FREEZE:** Freeze in a large, resealable plastic bag.
			THAW: Serve directly from the freezer, or thaw in the refrigerator for several hours before serving.

JUST SO BUSY!

English Muffin Breakfast Sandwiches • Roasted Tomato Soup with Thyme • Black Bean and
Roasted Chile Burritos • Oven-Fried Chicken • Classic Meat Loaf • Oatmeal Raisin Cookies

This plan is a general, non-event-specific freezer filler. These recipes are all easy to prep and quick to thaw, heat, and serve. They're also great for quick meals at home, or to pack along for breakfast on the go or lunch at your desk. Some of these recipes make enough servings for guests, like the Black Bean and Roasted Chile Burritos (serves 12) and Oven-Fried Chicken (serves 8). If you don't plan on company, simply store extra servings in the freezer for another day. And for a recipe like the Classic Meat Loaf that serves four, you can always double this to feed a bigger family. This meal plan can be accomplished in under 2 hours.

PREP

Preheat the oven to 350°F and lightly oil a muffin tin for the **English Muffin Breakfast Sandwiches**. Break the eggs into the muffin tin, season, and bake for 25 minutes. Meanwhile, cook the sausage, toast the muffins, and prepare the cheese slices. When the eggs are finished baking, remove from the oven and let cool to room temperature. Raise the oven temperature to 450°F.

Prep the tomatoes and garlic for roasting for **Roasted Tomato Soup with Thyme**. Roast for about 45 minutes, until soft.

While the tomatoes are roasting, assemble the **Black Bean and Roasted Chile Burritos**. Pack and freeze. [Black Bean and Roasted Chile Burritos are done.]

Assemble the English Muffin Breakfast Sandwiches, pack, and freeze. [English Muffin Breakfast Sandwiches are done.]

Purée the tomatoes with the remaining ingredients for the Roasted Tomato Soup with Thyme. Let cool to room temperature.

Prep and coat the chicken pieces for the **Oven-Fried Chicken**. Freeze on the baking sheet and transfer to a large, resealable plastic bag. [Oven-Fried Chicken is done.]

Combine the ingredients for the **Classic Meat Loaf** and form the mixture into two loaves. Pack and freeze. [Classic Meat Loaf is done.]

Mix together the ingredients for the **Oatmeal Raisin Cookies**. Form the cookie balls, freeze on a large baking sheet, and transfer to a large, resealable plastic bag. [Oatmeal Raisin Cookies are done.]

Pack and freeze the Roasted Tomato Soup with Thyme. [Roasted Tomato Soup with Thyme is done.]

ENGLISH MUFFIN BREAKFAST SANDWICHES

PAGE 49	SERVES 12	PREP 10 MINS	**FREEZE:** Wrap each sandwich individually in plastic wrap or aluminum foil, and freeze in a large, resealable plastic bag.
			THAW: To serve, microwave a plastic-wrapped frozen sandwich for about three minutes, or reheat a foil-wrapped frozen sandwich in a 350°F oven for about 35 minutes. Or thaw the sandwiches overnight in the refrigerator, then reheat for a minute in the microwave or about 15 minutes in a 350°F oven.

ROASTED TOMATO SOUP WITH THYME

PAGE 54	SERVES 6	PREP 10 MINS	**FREEZE:** Freeze the soup in single-serving storage containers or in two large, resealable plastic bags.
			THAW: To serve, thaw in the refrigerator overnight or in the microwave, and reheat either on the stovetop or in the microwave.

BLACK BEAN AND ROASTED CHILE BURRITOS

PAGE 70	SERVES 12	PREP 20 MINS	**FREEZE:** Wrap the burritos individually in plastic wrap and freeze.
			THAW: Wrap each burrito in a damp paper towel, then thaw in the microwave for about four minutes, turning once.

OVEN-FRIED CHICKEN

PAGE 108	SERVES 8	PREP 15 MINS	**FREEZE:** Freeze the coated chicken pieces on a baking sheet until solid, then transfer to one or two large, resealable plastic bags.
			THAW: To cook, bake from frozen in a 350°F oven for 50 to 60 minutes.

CLASSIC MEAT LOAF

PAGE 126	SERVES 4	PREP 10 MINS	**FREEZE:** Freeze the uncooked loaves tightly wrapped in plastic wrap or aluminum foil.
			THAW: Cook from frozen in a preheated 350°F oven for about 1½ hours, or thaw in the refrigerator for at least 24 hours, then cook in a 350°F oven for about one hour.

OATMEAL RAISIN COOKIES

PAGE 178	MAKES 4 DOZEN	PREP 15 MINS	**FREEZE:** Freeze the formed but unbaked cookies on a baking sheet until solid, then transfer to one or two large, resealable plastic bags.
			THAW: Bake from frozen in a 375°F oven on a parchment-lined baking sheet for 15 to 18 minutes.

FLUFFY WHOLE-WHEAT PUMPKIN PANCAKES (PAGE 41)

chapter three

BREAKFAST

TOASTED OAT, NUT, AND HONEY CEREAL BARS

MAKES 12 BARS • PREP TIME: 10 MINUTES • COOK TIME: 20 MINUTES

These crunchy-sweet breakfast bars are a perfect grab-and-go breakfast. I use walnuts and almonds, but you can choose any combination of nuts you like. Hazelnuts, cashews, peanuts, pecans, and pistachios all work well.

1½ cups (gluten-free) old-fashioned rolled oats
1 cup chopped walnuts
1 cup sliced almonds
½ cup honey
3 tablespoons light brown sugar
2 tablespoons unsalted butter, plus additional for preparing the baking dish
1½ teaspoons vanilla extract
¼ teaspoon kosher salt
1 cup crisp rice cereal

Preheat the oven to 350°F.

Line a baking sheet with aluminum foil.

Spread the oats, walnuts, and almonds out in an even layer on the prepared baking sheet, and toast in the oven for 7 minutes. Reduce the heat to 300°F.

Meanwhile, in a small saucepan, stir together the honey, sugar, 2 tablespoons butter, vanilla, salt, and rice cereal. Heat, stirring frequently, until the butter melts and the sugar dissolves.

In a large mixing bowl, stir together the oat-and-nut mixture with the honey-and-butter mixture.

Use the aluminum foil from the baking sheet to line a 9-by-13-inch baking dish. Lightly butter the foil, then spread the oat-and-nut mixture out in the dish, pressing it into an even layer. Bake for 20 minutes. Remove from the oven, and set the baking dish on a wire rack to cool completely. Using the foil lining the dish as a sling, lift the bars out of the baking dish and cut into 12 bars.

GLUTEN-FREE: Use gluten-free oats.

DAIRY-FREE: Substitute coconut oil for the butter.

TO REFRIGERATE: Arrange the bars in a single layer in an airtight container, and store in the refrigerator for up to a week. Bring to room temperature before serving.

TO FREEZE: Wrap the bars individually in plastic wrap or foil, and store in a large, resealable plastic bag in the freezer for up to three months. Thaw overnight on the countertop, and serve at room temperature.

VEGETARIAN

BLUEBERRY-COCONUT GRANOLA BARS

MAKES 12 BARS • PREP TIME: 10 MINUTES • COOK TIME: 40 MINUTES

Chock-full of cinnamon, blueberries, and coconut, these simple granola bars are best served with a glass of milk or a bowl of fruit-sweetened yogurt for a well-rounded breakfast. Or grab one on the way out the door for a healthy breakfast on the go.

3 tablespoons butter, plus additional for preparing the baking dish

½ cup honey

3 tablespoons light brown sugar

1 tablespoon cinnamon

¼ teaspoon kosher salt

1½ cups old-fashioned rolled oats

1 cup unsweetened shredded coconut

1½ cups blueberries

Preheat the oven to 350°F.

Line a 9-by-13-inch baking dish with aluminum foil and lightly butter the foil.

In a small saucepan, combine the butter, honey, brown sugar, cinnamon, and salt, and bring to a boil over medium-high heat. Let boil for about 2 minutes, and remove from the heat.

In a large mixing bowl, combine the oats, coconut, and blueberries. Pour the honey mixture over the dry ingredients and stir gently until well combined. Transfer the mixture to the prepared baking dish and press it into an even layer. Bake in the preheated oven for 40 minutes.

Remove from the oven and let cool completely on a wire rack. Use the aluminum foil to lift the bars out of the baking dish, and cut into 12 bars.

GLUTEN-FREE: Use gluten-free oats.

DAIRY-FREE: Substitute coconut oil for butter.

TO REFRIGERATE: Wrap the bars individually in plastic wrap or foil, and store in a large, resealable plastic bag in the refrigerator for up to 2 weeks. Bring to room temperature before serving.

TO FREEZE: Wrap the bars individually in plastic wrap or foil, and store in a large, resealable plastic bag in the freezer for up to three months. Thaw overnight on the countertop, and serve at room temperature.

VEGETARIAN

MAPLE-PECAN PUMPKIN BREAD

MAKES 12 SLICES • PREP TIME: 10 MINUTES • COOK TIME: 35 MINUTES

This moist, slightly sweet pumpkin bread is studded with crunchy pecans. I love to make it as a back-to-school breakfast or snack. Eat it plain or toasted, spread with cream cheese or butter mixed with maple syrup.

½ cup cooking oil (melted coconut oil, sunflower seed, etc.), plus additional for preparing the loaf pan

1½ cups whole-wheat flour

2 teaspoons pumpkin pie spice

1 teaspoon baking soda

½ teaspoon baking powder

¼ teaspoon fine sea salt

2 large eggs

½ cup maple syrup

1 teaspoon vanilla

1 cup pumpkin purée

½ cup chopped pecans

Preheat the oven to 350°F.

Lightly oil a 9-by-5-inch loaf pan.

Combine the flour, pumpkin pie spice, baking soda, baking powder, and salt in a large mixing bowl. Add the eggs, oil, maple syrup, and vanilla, and whisk to combine. Gently fold in the pumpkin purée and pecans.

Pour the batter into the prepared loaf pan. Bake in the preheated oven for about 35 minutes, until a toothpick inserted into the center comes out clean. Remove from the oven and let cool in the pan for 10 minutes before slicing. Serve warm, at room temperature, or lightly toasted.

TO REFRIGERATE: Wrap the loaf tightly in plastic wrap, and store in the refrigerator for up to a week. Bring to room temperature or toast before serving.

TO FREEZE: Cut the loaf into 12 slices. Wrap each slice individually in plastic wrap, or place squares of parchment between the slices, then wrap the whole loaf tightly in plastic wrap. Store in the freezer for up to three months. To serve, thaw at room temperature for an hour or two, or toast lightly.

VEGETARIAN

DAIRY-FREE

COCOA-BANANA BAKED OATMEAL CUPS

MAKES 12 CUPS • PREP TIME: 10 MINUTES • COOK TIME: 30 MINUTES

These miniature oatmeal breakfast cakes let you take your bowl of oatmeal to go in the morning. Chock-full of flavor, they give you all the health benefits of oatmeal, but in the handy form of a muffin.

¼ cup oil (coconut, sunflower seed, etc.), plus additional for preparing the muffin tin

3 cups old-fashioned rolled oats

1 teaspoon cinnamon

2 tablespoons unsweetened cocoa powder

1 teaspoon baking powder

¼ teaspoon fine sea salt

2 large eggs

¼ cup honey

2 ripe bananas, mashed

2 teaspoons vanilla extract

1 cup milk

Preheat the oven to 350°F.

Lightly oil a muffin tin.

In a medium mixing bowl, stir together the oats, cinnamon, cocoa powder, baking powder, and salt.

In a separate bowl, whisk together the eggs, honey, bananas, and vanilla until smooth. Whisk in the oil and milk. Pour this mixture into the dry ingredients, and stir until the dry ingredients are fully moistened.

Spoon the batter into the prepared muffin tin, dividing equally, and bake in the preheated oven for about 30 minutes, until the tops begin to brown. Remove the muffin tin from the oven and let cool for 5 minutes before removing the oatmeal cups from the tin. Serve immediately or let cool completely before storing.

GLUTEN-FREE: Use gluten-free oats.

DAIRY-FREE: Use nondairy milk substitute instead of milk.

TO REFRIGERATE: Store in an airtight container in the refrigerator for up to a week. To serve, place the oatmeal cup on a microwave-safe dish, and microwave on high for about two minutes.

TO FREEZE: Wrap each baked oatmeal cup tightly in plastic wrap, and store them all together in a large, resealable plastic bag in the freezer for up to three months. To serve, place an unwrapped cup on a microwave-safe dish, and microwave on high for about two minutes.

TIP: Place a cup of water in the microwave alongside the oatmeal cup. This will keep the oatmeal cup moist as it reheats.

VEGETARIAN

COCONUT BROWN RICE PUDDING

This is a breakfast for those who love dessert. It's only lightly sweetened with brown sugar (you can substitute honey or maple syrup, if you prefer), but the combination of coconut milk and cinnamon makes for a decadent flavor. Using brown rice instead of white adds both a slight nutty taste and a satisfying chewiness, plus vitamins and fiber that will keep you feeling full all morning.

1 cup short-grain brown rice

2 cups almond milk

1 (15-ounce) can light coconut milk

¼ cup light brown sugar

1 teaspoon vanilla extract

1 teaspoon cinnamon

½ cup raisins (optional)

In a medium saucepan, combine the rice with 2 cups of water and bring to a boil. Reduce the heat to low, cover, and simmer for 30 minutes. Remove from the heat, and let sit, covered, for 10 minutes.

Stir the almond milk and coconut milk into the cooked rice along with the brown sugar, vanilla, cinnamon, and raisins (if using). Bring to a simmer over medium-high heat. Reduce the heat to low, cover, and simmer, stirring frequently, until the rice is tender and the mixture is creamy, about 30 minutes. Remove from the heat, and let cool before serving.

TIP: To make this recipe in a slow cooker, combine the rice, almond milk, and coconut milk with the sugar, cinnamon, and raisins (if using) in a lightly oiled slow cooker. Cover and cook on high for 3 ½ to 4 hours, until the rice is tender and the mixture is creamy. Stir in the vanilla and let cool.

TO REFRIGERATE: Transfer the pudding to a large bowl or individual serving dishes. Cover with plastic wrap, pressing the plastic onto the surface of the pudding, and refrigerate for up to three days. Serve chilled or at room temperature.

TO FREEZE: Spoon the pudding into a lightly oiled muffin tin, dividing equally among 10 muffin cups, then cover with plastic wrap and freeze. Once puddings are frozen, pop them out of the muffin tin, wrap individually in plastic wrap, and store in one large, resealable plastic bag for up to three months. Thaw overnight in the refrigerator or in the microwave, and serve chilled or at room temperature.

VEGAN

GLUTEN-FREE

DAIRY-FREE

FLUFFY WHOLE-WHEAT PUMPKIN PANCAKES

Adding pumpkin purée to these whole-wheat pancakes makes them incredibly moist. Top them with chopped fruit and yogurt for a satisfying, well-balanced breakfast.

2 cups whole-wheat flour

2 tablespoons baking powder

1 teaspoon cinnamon

½ teaspoon fine sea salt

2 cups milk

⅔ cup pumpkin purée

2 large eggs

¼ cup maple syrup or brown sugar

1 teaspoon vanilla extract

¼ cup cooking oil (melted coconut oil, sunflower seed, etc.), plus additional for the skillet

In a medium mixing bowl, stir together the flour, baking powder, cinnamon, and salt.

In a separate mixing bowl, whisk together the milk, pumpkin, eggs, maple syrup or brown sugar, vanilla, and ¼ cup oil. Add the wet ingredients to the dry ingredients, and stir until just combined.

Lightly oil a large skillet and heat over medium-high heat. Spoon the batter, ¼ cup at a time, into the skillet and cook for 2 to 3 minutes, until small bubbles on the top of the pancakes pop and leave holes. Flip over and cook on the second side for 1 to 2 minutes more, until golden brown.

Repeat until all of the batter has been used, adding more oil to the skillet if needed. Serve immediately, or let cool to room temperature before storing.

DAIRY-FREE: Use a nondairy milk substitute instead of milk.

TO REFRIGERATE: Place the pancakes on a plate, cover with aluminum foil or plastic wrap, and refrigerate for up to three days. Before serving, reheat briefly in the microwave (on a microwave-safe plate) or in a 350°F oven (wrapped in aluminum foil).

TO FREEZE: Arrange the pancakes in a single layer on a large baking sheet, cover with plastic wrap, and freeze. (Alternately, stack them with squares of parchment paper in between them so they don't stick together.) Once pancakes are frozen, transfer to a large, resealable plastic bag, and freeze for up to three months. To serve, reheat frozen pancakes in the microwave (on a microwave-safe plate) for about two minutes, or in a 350°F oven (wrapped in aluminum foil) for 5 to 10 minutes.

VEGETARIAN

GLUTEN-FREE BLUEBERRY PANCAKE MUFFINS

These portable pancake muffins are made with almond flour, giving them a boost of both protein and heart-healthy monounsaturated fats. The best part is that they taste just like blueberry pancakes but are much easier to grab as you dash out the door in the morning.

2 tablespoons unsalted butter, melted, plus
    additional for preparing the muffin tin
⅓ cup plain yogurt
1 tablespoon maple syrup
1 teaspoon vanilla extract
¼ teaspoon apple-cider vinegar
1¾ cups almond flour
½ teaspoon baking soda
¼ teaspoon fine sea salt
3 large eggs
½ cup fresh or frozen (thawed and drained)
    blueberries

Preheat the oven to 350°F.

Grease 8 muffin cups in a 12-cup muffin tin with butter. Set aside.

In a blender, combine the melted butter, yogurt, maple syrup, vanilla, and vinegar, and pulse briefly to combine. Add the almond flour, baking soda, and salt, and blend for about 15 seconds, until well combined. Add the eggs and blend on low speed for another 15 seconds, and then on high speed for 20 to 30 seconds longer until the eggs are fully incorporated. Stir in the blueberries.

Pour the batter into the muffin tin, dividing equally among the 8 prepared cups. Bake in the preheated oven for 15 to 18 minutes, until the tops are light golden brown and a toothpick inserted into the center of a muffin comes out clean. Remove the muffin tin from the oven and let cool for a few minutes before removing the muffins from the tin. Serve immediately or cool to room temperature before storing.

DAIRY-FREE/PALEO: Substitute coconut milk yogurt for yogurt and coconut oil for butter.

TO REFRIGERATE: Wrap the muffins in plastic wrap or aluminum foil and store in the refrigerator for up to three days. To serve, reheat on a microwave-safe plate in the microwave for about a minute, or wrapped in foil in a 350°F oven for 5 to 10 minutes.

TO FREEZE: Wrap the muffins individually in plastic wrap or aluminum foil, and store them in a large, resealable plastic bag in the freezer for up to three months. Before serving, reheat on a microwave-safe plate in the microwave for about 2 minutes, or wrapped in foil in a 350°F oven for 10 to 15 minutes.

VEGETARIAN

GLUTEN-FREE

WHOLE-GRAIN BUTTERMILK-RASPBERRY MUFFINS

These oat-and-wheat muffins are fluffy, moist, and full of fiber and the essential nutrients that come from whole grains. Buttermilk adds a bit of tang to balance the sweetness of the berries. While you can certainly opt for fresh berries in this recipe, frozen berries are every bit as good.

⅓ cup cooking oil (coconut, sunflower seed, etc.),
    plus additional for preparing the muffin tin
1 cup old-fashioned oats
1 cup buttermilk
½ cup packed brown sugar
1 large egg
1 cup whole-wheat flour
1 teaspoon baking soda
1 teaspoon cinnamon
¼ teaspoon fine sea salt
1 cup fresh or frozen (thawed) raspberries

Preheat the oven to 400°F.

Lightly oil a muffin tin.

In small mixing bowl, combine the oats and buttermilk and let sit for a few minutes. Meanwhile, in a large mixing bowl, whisk together the oil, sugar, and egg. Add the flour, baking soda, cinnamon, and salt, and mix until just combined.

Stir in the buttermilk-oat mixture, then gently fold in the berries. Spoon the batter into the prepared muffin tin.

Bake in the preheated oven for 15 to 20 minutes, until the tops are golden brown. Remove from the oven and let cool for 5 minutes before removing the muffins from the tin. Serve warm or let cool to room temperature before storing.

TIP: You can substitute any berries for the raspberries. Try blueberries, blackberries, or boysenberries.

TO REFRIGERATE: Cover and refrigerate for up to a week. Bring to room temperature before serving.

TO FREEZE: Arrange the muffins on a baking sheet and freeze, then transfer to a large, resealable plastic bag and keep in the freezer for up to three months. Before serving, thaw muffins completely at room temperature, or reheat, wrapped in foil in a 350°F oven, or in the microwave.

VEGETARIAN

WHOLE-WHEAT BREAD PUDDING WITH ALMOND BUTTER AND BERRIES

SERVES 12 • PREP TIME: 10 MINUTES • COOK TIME: 40 MINUTES

For this pudding, feel free to use any combination of berries you like. Try substituting peanut butter for the almond butter to create a bread pudding that incorporates those classic, irresistible peanut butter and jelly flavors.

Oil or butter for preparing the baking dish
4 large eggs
2 cups almond milk
1 cup almond butter
½ cup honey
2 tablespoons unsalted butter, melted
6 slices whole-wheat sandwich bread, torn into
    bite-size pieces
1 cup fresh or frozen (thawed) berries
    (raspberries, blueberries, blackberries, or a
    combination)

Preheat the oven to 350°F.

Lightly oil or butter an 8-by-8-inch baking dish.

In a large mixing bowl, whisk together the eggs, almond milk, almond butter, honey, and butter. Add the bread and berries, and toss to combine. Transfer the mixture to the prepared baking dish, spreading it out into an even layer.

Bake in the preheated oven for 35 to 40 minutes, until the top turns golden brown and springs back when lightly pressed. Serve warm or let cool to room temperature before storing.

GLUTEN-FREE: Use whole-grain, gluten-free bread.

TIP: You can make individual bread puddings by dividing the egg and bread mixture into the cups of a lightly oiled muffin tin. Reduce the baking time by 5 to 10 minutes.

TO REFRIGERATE: Cover and refrigerate for up to three days. To serve, reheat, covered with aluminum foil, in a 350°F oven for about 10 minutes.

TO FREEZE: Cut into squares and wrap individually in plastic wrap. Store the wrapped squares in a large, resealable plastic bag for up to three months. To reheat, thaw in the refrigerator overnight, and then heat, wrapped in aluminum foil, in a 350°F oven for about 10 minutes.

VEGETARIAN

SWEET POTATO HASH AND EGGS

Sweet potatoes are one of the most nutritious vegetables around. They also taste great and add a burst of bright orange color to a simple breakfast hash. This hash is prepared by roasting the vegetables together in the oven, making the cooking practically hands-free.

2 pounds sweet potatoes, cut into 1-inch cubes

1 red bell pepper, seeded and diced

1 onion, diced

4 tablespoons olive oil, divided

1½ teaspoons kosher salt, divided

¾ teaspoon freshly ground black pepper, divided

12 large eggs

4 ounces shredded Cheddar cheese

3 scallions, chopped

Preheat the oven to 425°F.

On a large baking sheet, toss the sweet potatoes, bell pepper, and onion together and then drizzle with 3 tablespoons of olive oil. Season with 1 teaspoon of salt and ½ teaspoon of pepper, and then toss to coat evenly. Transfer half the vegetables to a second large baking sheet.

Roast in the preheated oven for 30 to 40 minutes, rotating the pans and stirring the vegetables halfway through, until the potatoes are tender and golden.

Meanwhile, whisk the eggs with the remaining ½ teaspoon of salt and the remaining ¼ teaspoon of pepper in a large bowl. Heat the remaining tablespoon of olive oil in a large skillet over medium heat. Add the eggs and cook, stirring frequently, until just barely set, about 2 minutes. Transfer the eggs to a plate.

To serve immediately, pile the hash into individual serving bowls and top with the eggs, shredded cheese, and scallions.

TO REFRIGERATE: Allow the components to cool to room temperature. Divide the hash equally into 12 storage containers, and top each with equal portions of the eggs, cheese, and scallions. Store in the refrigerator for up to two days. To serve, reheat in the microwave.

TO FREEZE: Allow the components to cool to room temperature. Divide the hash equally into 12 freezer-safe storage containers, and top with equal portions of the eggs, cheese, and scallions. Store in the freezer for up to three months. To serve, reheat from frozen in the microwave on 50 percent power, stirring every 30 seconds, until heated through.

VEGETARIAN

GREEK-STYLE FRITTATA WITH FETA CHEESE

Frittatas are some of the best make-ahead meals, because they're easy to prepare and can be served hot, warm, or at room temperature—and the possible variations are endless. In this one, feta cheese and oregano provide a distinctive Greek-inspired slant.

6 large eggs

¾ cup crumbled feta cheese

½ cup milk

1 tablespoon minced fresh oregano or 1 teaspoon dried oregano

½ teaspoon kosher salt

¼ teaspoon freshly ground black pepper

2 tablespoons olive oil

½ onion, diced

1 large tomato, diced

1½ cups chopped spinach

Preheat the broiler.

In a medium bowl, whisk together the eggs, feta, milk, oregano, salt, and pepper.

Heat the olive oil in a large skillet over medium-high heat. Add the onion and cook, stirring, until it begins to soften, about 3 minutes. Add the tomato and spinach and cook, stirring frequently, for about 3 minutes more, until the onions are soft, the tomato has cooked down, and the spinach has wilted. Stir in the egg mixture and cook for about 5 minutes, until the egg sets on the bottom and sides but is still runny on top.

Transfer the skillet to the broiler, and cook until the top and center are fully set and turn light brown, about 4 minutes more.

Remove from the oven, let rest for 5 minutes, and then slice into wedges. Serve immediately or let cool to room temperature before storing.

TO REFRIGERATE: Cover tightly with plastic wrap and refrigerate for up to three days. To serve, bring to room temperature or reheat in the microwave.

TO FREEZE: Wrap the entire frittata tightly in plastic wrap, or slice the frittata into wedges, wrapping each wedge tightly in plastic wrap and storing them in a large, resealable plastic bag. Freeze for up to three months. To serve, thaw the frittata in the refrigerator for 24 hours, then reheat in the microwave or bring to room temperature.

TIP: After defrosting the frittata in the refrigerator for an hour or two, unwrap it, place on a plate, and recover with plastic wrap. This will help release condensation so the frittata doesn't become watery during thawing.

VEGETARIAN

GLUTEN-FREE

READY-TO-COOK HAM, CHEDDAR, AND GREEN CHILE QUICHE

SERVES 8 • PREP TIME: 10 MINUTES • COOK TIME: 50 MINUTES

Quiche is so easy! Just mix the raw ingredients and freeze to cook for the next time you need to guarantee a great meal. You can cook the filling in a store-bought or homemade pastry crust, without a crust at all, or with shredded or thinly sliced white or sweet potatoes in place of a crust.

2 cups milk

1 (7-ounce) can fire-roasted diced
    green chiles, drained

4 eggs, beaten

1 cup diced ham

½ cup all-purpose flour

4 scallions, sliced

1 cup Cheddar cheese, shredded

2 teaspoons baking powder

½ teaspoon kosher salt

¼ teaspoon freshly ground black pepper

1 deep-dish pie crust (optional)

In a large mixing bowl, stir together the milk, chiles, eggs, ham, flour, scallions, cheese, baking powder, salt, and pepper. To refrigerate or freeze, skip ahead to the storage instructions below.

To cook, preheat the oven to 350°F and pour the egg mixture into a deep-dish pie crust (if using) or deep-dish pie plate. Bake until the top is lightly browned and the center is set, about 50 minutes if baking in a crust or 40 minutes if crustless.

TIP: To ensure a crispy crust, parbake the crust for 13 to 15 minutes, until it's lightly golden brown, before adding the filling.

TO REFRIGERATE: Cover and refrigerate the egg mixture for up to two days. To serve, follow the cooking instructions above.

TO FREEZE: Transfer the egg mixture to a large, resealable plastic bag. Remove as much air as possible from the bag, lay the bag flat on a baking sheet, and place in the freezer until frozen solid. Store up to three months. To serve, thaw in the refrigerator for 24 hours. Follow the cooking instructions above.

EGG-AND-CHEESE MINI BREAKFAST TOSTADA CUPS

MAKES 12 • PREP TIME: 10 MINUTES • COOK TIME: 30 MINUTES

Eggs loaded with black beans, veggies, and cheese and baked in crispy corn tortilla cups are as adorable as they are delicious. Serve these topped with salsa, sour cream, or avocado for some extra Mexican-inspired flair.

Cooking oil spray

12 small (5- to 6-inch) corn tortillas

12 eggs

¾ cup whole milk

½ teaspoon kosher salt

½ teaspoon freshly ground black pepper

1½ cups shredded Cheddar cheese, divided

1 large red bell pepper, seeded and diced

1 onion, diced

1 cup canned black beans, rinsed and drained

Preheat the oven to 350°F.

Spray a muffin tin with cooking oil spray.

Wrap the tortillas, 6 at a time, in damp paper towels, and microwave on high for 30 seconds to make them pliable. Put the tortillas into the muffin tin, pressing them down to form them into cup shapes. Bake in the preheated oven until the tortillas are lightly brown and crisp, 10 to 15 minutes.

Meanwhile, whisk together the eggs, milk, salt, and pepper. Stir in 1 cup of cheese and the bell pepper, onion, and beans.

Spoon the egg mixture into the tortilla cups in the muffin tin, dividing equally. Bake in the preheated oven for 10 minutes. Sprinkle the remaining ½ cup of cheese over the eggs and return the tortilla cups to the oven. Bake for another 5 minutes or so, until the cheese is bubbly and the tortillas are golden brown and crisp. Serve immediately or let cool to room temperature before storing.

TO REFRIGERATE: Store covered in the refrigerator for up to five days. To serve, reheat in a 350°F oven for 10 minutes or until heated through.

TO FREEZE: Wrap each tortilla cup tightly in plastic wrap and store them all in a large, resealable plastic bag in the freezer for up to three months. To serve, defrost in the refrigerator overnight, then reheat in a 350°F oven for 10 minutes or until heated through.

VEGETARIAN

GLUTEN-FREE

ENGLISH MUFFIN BREAKFAST SANDWICHES

MAKES 12 • PREP TIME: 10 MINUTES • COOK TIME: 40 MINUTES

Using whole-wheat muffins and healthier breakfast sausage, these easy grab-and-go breakfast sandwiches are much better than their fast-food counterparts. Heat them from frozen in the microwave, and you've got a tasty, hot breakfast in three minutes.

Cooking oil spray
12 large eggs
½ teaspoon kosher salt
½ teaspoon freshly ground black pepper
12 whole-wheat English muffins
12 turkey breakfast sausage patties
12 slices cheese (Cheddar, Swiss, or Jack)

Preheat the oven to 350°F.

Coat a muffin tin lightly with cooking oil spray.

Crack one egg into each of the 12 cups of the prepared muffin tin, and use a small knife to break each yolk so that it spreads out a bit. Sprinkle the salt and pepper over the eggs, dividing equally. Bake in the preheated oven for 25 to 30 minutes, until the whites and yolks are set. (If you're planning to serve them right away, you might want to reduce the cook time for a runnier yolk.)

While the eggs are baking, cook the sausage patties in a skillet until lightly browned on both sides, about 5 minutes.

Remove the muffin tin from the oven, and let the eggs cool for a few minutes. Meanwhile, toast the English muffins.

Place 1 slice of cheese on the bottom half of each muffin. Top with a sausage patty and a cooked egg, then finish with the other half of the muffin. Serve immediately or let come to room temperature before storing.

VEGETARIAN: Use vegetarian breakfast sausage patties.

DAIRY-FREE: Omit the cheese.

TO REFRIGERATE: Wrap each sandwich individually in plastic wrap or aluminum foil, and store in the refrigerator for up to three days. To serve, reheat in the microwave for about a minute.

TO FREEZE: Wrap each sandwich individually in plastic wrap (if planning to reheat in the microwave) or aluminum foil (if planning to reheat in the oven), and store in a large, resealable plastic bag in the freezer for up to three months. To serve, microwave a plastic-wrapped frozen sandwich for about three minutes, or reheat a foil-wrapped frozen sandwich in a 350°F oven for about 35 minutes. You can also thaw the sandwiches overnight in the refrigerator, and then reheat either for 1 minute in the microwave or about 15 minutes in a 350°F oven.

SLOW COOKER FRENCH ONION SOUP (PAGE 61)

SOUPS AND STEWS

GINGERY CARROT-AND-APPLE SOUP

MAKES ABOUT 8 CUPS • PREP TIME: 10 MINUTES • COOK TIME: 30 MINUTES

This bright orange soup is guaranteed to brighten up even the darkest winter night. Its gingery kick is set off by lots of lovely sweetness from the carrots and apples. I like to serve it accompanied by grilled cheese sandwiches or a slice of quiche for an easy meal.

2 tablespoons olive oil
1 large onion, diced
3 garlic cloves, minced
3 tablespoons grated fresh ginger
2 medium apples, cored and diced
2 ¼ pounds carrots, peeled and chopped
6 cups vegetable broth
¾ teaspoon kosher salt

Heat the olive oil in a large pot over medium heat. Add the onion and cook, stirring frequently, for about 5 minutes, until soft and translucent. Reduce the heat to low, add the garlic and ginger, and continue to cook, stirring, for 2 more minutes. Stir in the apple and carrots and cook for 3 minutes more.

Stir in the vegetable broth and salt, and bring to a boil. Reduce the heat to medium-low, and let simmer until the apples and carrots are tender, about 20 minutes.

Using an immersion blender, or in batches in a countertop blender, blend the soup until it is smooth. Return to the pot and reheat if necessary to serve immediately, or let cool to room temperature before storing.

GLUTEN-FREE: Use gluten-free broth.

TIP: Any type of apple will work for this recipe. I like to use a tart-sweet green apple like Granny Smith.

TO REFRIGERATE: Cover and refrigerate for up to a week. Reheat in the microwave or on the stovetop before serving.

TO FREEZE: Transfer the soup to a half-gallon-size resealable plastic bag or to two quart-size resealable plastic bags, dividing the soup equally. Remove as much air as possible, and lay the bag or bags on a baking sheet to freeze. Alternatively, transfer the soup to single-serving freezer containers (ideally microwave-safe) and freeze. The soup will keep in the freezer for up to three months. To serve, thaw in the microwave or in a bowl of hot water until it is soft enough to remove from the bag, then reheat in the microwave or in a saucepan on the stovetop.

PALEO

VEGAN

DAIRY-FREE

TUSCAN-STYLE WHITE BEAN AND KALE SOUP

SERVES 8 • PREP TIME: 10 MINUTES • COOK TIME: 30 MINUTES

This Italian-style vegetable soup is thickened with mashed beans and loaded with healthy kale, making it both filling and good for you. Serve it with crusty bread for dunking, and you've got a perfect, hearty meal for a chilly night.

2 (15-ounce) cans cannellini beans, rinsed and drained, divided

3 tablespoons olive oil

4 garlic cloves, thinly sliced

1½ cups diced carrots

1½ cups diced celery

¼ teaspoon salt, divided

½ teaspoon freshly ground black pepper

1 pound kale, trimmed and cut into 2-inch-wide ribbons

8 cups vegetable broth

1 (14-ounce) can diced tomatoes, drained

In a bowl, mash one can of beans into a paste.

Heat the oil in a stockpot or Dutch oven over medium heat. Add the garlic and cook, stirring, for 1 minute.

Stir in the carrots, celery, salt, and pepper. Cook, stirring frequently, for 4 minutes.

Stir in the kale, cover, and cook, stirring occasionally, for about 5 minutes, until the kale is tender.

Add the broth, tomatoes, mashed beans, and the remaining can of whole beans. Bring to a simmer, cover, reduce the heat to low, and cook, stirring occasionally, for about 20 minutes, until the vegetables are tender. Serve immediately, or cool to room temperature before storing.

GLUTEN-FREE: Use gluten-free broth.

TIP: For best results, allow this soup to sit for at least a few hours before serving. It's even better the following day.

TO REFRIGERATE: Cover and refrigerate the soup for up to two days. To serve, reheat on the stovetop or in the microwave.

TO FREEZE: Portion the soup into single-serving storage containers or resealable plastic bags (either one large bag or two small ones), and freeze for up to six months. To serve, thaw in the refrigerator overnight or in the microwave, then reheat.

VEGAN

DAIRY-FREE

ROASTED TOMATO SOUP WITH THYME

SERVES 6 • PREP TIME: 10 MINUTES • COOK TIME: 45 MINUTES

Roasting tomatoes along with onions, garlic, and thyme gives them a deep, rich sweetness. This soup provides the perfect match for a classic grilled cheese sandwich—or try serving it with a simple green salad, crusty bread, and cheese.

3 pounds Roma tomatoes, halved, stem
    ends removed
1 large onion, coarsely chopped
8 medium garlic cloves, peeled
2 tablespoons olive oil
1 teaspoon kosher salt
1 teaspoon freshly ground black pepper
5 sprigs fresh thyme
4 cups vegetable broth
Juice of 1 lemon

Preheat the oven to 450°F.

On a large, rimmed baking sheet, toss the tomatoes, onion, and garlic with olive oil, salt, pepper, and thyme. Spread everything out in an even layer, turning the tomatoes cut-side up.

Roast in the preheated oven for about 45 minutes, stirring occasionally, until the tomatoes and onions are very soft.

Transfer the roasted vegetables and their juices into a stockpot (discard the thyme stems, leaving any leaves that have fallen off), add the broth, and purée with an immersion blender or in batches in a countertop blender. Stir in the lemon juice. To serve immediately, bring to a simmer in a stockpot over medium heat.

GLUTEN-FREE: Use gluten-free broth.

TIP: For a richer soup, stir in ½ cup of half-and-half or heavy cream just before serving.

TO REFRIGERATE: Store, covered, in the refrigerator for up to three days. Reheat on the stovetop or in the microwave before serving.

TO FREEZE: Portion the soup into single-serving storage containers or resealable plastic bags (either one large bag or two small ones), and freeze for up to six months. To serve, thaw in the refrigerator overnight or in the microwave, then reheat.

PALEO

VEGAN

DAIRY-FREE

CURRY NOODLE SOUP WITH SMOKED TOFU

SERVES 4 • PREP TIME: 10 MINUTES • COOK TIME: 20 MINUTES

This simple soup is flavored with Thai curry paste. Strips of smoked tofu, found in many markets or health food stores, give it a boost of protein and a nice undercurrent of smoky flavor. If you can't find smoked tofu, substitute baked tofu or plain, firm tofu.

2 tablespoons cooking oil

1 shallot, thinly sliced

2 garlic cloves, minced

1 pound smoked tofu, cut into strips

2 to 4 tablespoons Thai red curry paste

1 tablespoon brown sugar

1 (15-ounce) can coconut milk

4 cups vegetable broth

2 tablespoons fish sauce

8 ounces thin rice noodles or other Asian noodles (such as udon)

Heat the oil in a stockpot or Dutch oven over medium-high heat. Add the shallot and garlic, and cook, stirring, until the shallot is soft, about 4 minutes.

Add the tofu and cook, stirring, for about 2 minutes, until the tofu begins to brown. Add the curry paste and cook, stirring, for about 1 minute, until it begins to darken.

Stir in the brown sugar and coconut milk and bring to a simmer. Add the broth and fish sauce and simmer, uncovered, for about 15 minutes, until the broth thickens slightly.

Meanwhile, cook the noodles according to the package directions.

If serving immediately, divide the noodles among the serving bowls, and ladle the hot soup over the top. Serve hot. If you are making the soup ahead, let the soup and noodles cool to room temperature separately.

GLUTEN-FREE: Use gluten-free broth and noodles.

VEGETARIAN/VEGAN: Substitute soy sauce or tamari for the fish sauce.

TIP: Thai red curry pastes vary widely in heat level, so start with a little and add more to taste.

TO REFRIGERATE: Store the noodles and soup in separate containers, covered, in the refrigerator, for up to three days. To serve, reheat the soup and noodles separately, either in the microwave or on the stovetop, and serve as above.

TO FREEZE: Portion the soup into single-serving storage containers or resealable plastic bags (either one large bag or two small ones), and freeze for up to six months. Store the noodles in a separate resealable plastic bag, or, if storing soup in individual servings, divide the noodles into an equal number of servings and store in small, resealable plastic bags. To serve, thaw both the soup and noodles in the refrigerator overnight or in the microwave, then reheat, separately, in the microwave or on the stovetop. Serve as directed above.

DAIRY-FREE

55

SOUPS AND STEWS

CORN AND SHRIMP CHOWDER

SERVES 4 • PREP TIME: 10 MINUTES • COOK TIME: 30 MINUTES

This simple chowder is seasoned with the heady flavors of garlic, onions, and smoked paprika. Potatoes thicken the broth, producing a satisfying one-bowl meal. For a richer soup, stir in a bit of heavy cream or half-and-half just before serving.

4 tablespoons butter, divided
1 pound shrimp, peeled, deveined, and chopped
1 onion, diced
2 celery ribs, diced
4 garlic cloves, minced
1½ tablespoons smoked paprika
4 cups chicken or seafood broth
1 pound Yukon gold potatoes, finely diced
2½ cups fresh or frozen corn kernels
¾ teaspoon kosher salt

In a stockpot or large Dutch oven, melt 1 tablespoon of butter over medium-high heat. Add the shrimp and cook, stirring occasionally, until they become opaque, about 4 minutes. Transfer the shrimp to a plate.

Add the remaining 3 tablespoons of butter to the pot along with the onion and celery. Cook, stirring frequently, for 4 minutes. Add the garlic and cook, stirring, for about 2 minutes more.

Stir in the smoked paprika, broth, potatoes, corn, and salt, and bring to a boil. Reduce the heat so that the soup is simmering. Simmer, uncovered, for 15 to 20 minutes, until the potatoes are tender.

Chop the cooked shrimp into bite-size pieces, and stir them into the soup. Simmer for a few minutes more, just until the shrimp is heated through. Serve immediately or let cool to room temperature before storing.

DAIRY-FREE: Substitute olive oil or coconut oil for the butter.

TIP: If you plan to freeze the soup, cook just until the potatoes are barely tender. They continue to cook during reheating, so slightly undercooking them will help prevent the soup from turning to mush.

TO REFRIGERATE: Transfer the soup to a storage container, cover, and refrigerate for up to two days. To serve, reheat the soup either in the microwave or on the stovetop.

TO FREEZE: Portion the soup into single-serving storage containers or into resealable plastic bags (one large one, two medium-sized ones, or several small ones), and freeze for up to three months. To serve, thaw the soup in the refrigerator overnight or in a bowl of cold water for about an hour. Reheat either in the microwave or on the stovetop.

THE HEALTHY MAKE-AHEAD COOKBOOK

SEAFOOD STEW

SERVES 6 TO 8 • PREP TIME: 10 MINUTES • COOK TIME: 45 MINUTES

A simple tomato broth provides a terrific base for a seafood stew. Using frozen seafood makes this dish unbelievably easy to prepare—and easy to keep in the freezer, too. Serve crusty garlic bread alongside this stew for a hearty meal.

2 tablespoons olive oil

1 onion, diced

4 garlic cloves, minced

2 teaspoons dried oregano

1½ teaspoons kosher salt

1 teaspoon freshly ground black pepper

1 (28-ounce) can tomato purée

6 cups chicken or seafood broth

2 pounds frozen seafood (shrimp, scallops, squid, clams, cod, etc.)

Heat the oil in a stockpot or Dutch oven over medium-high heat. Add the onion and garlic, and cook, stirring frequently, until softened, about 5 minutes.

Add the oregano, salt, and pepper, then stir in the tomato purée and broth, and bring to a boil. Reduce the heat to low, cover, and simmer for 30 minutes.

If you intend to serve the stew immediately or to refrigerate it now with plans to eat it in the next couple of days, add the frozen seafood and let it simmer, uncovered, until it is just cooked through, for 8 to 10 minutes. Serve immediately.

GLUTEN-FREE: Use gluten-free broth.

TIP: Use any type of seafood you enjoy most, such as shrimp, scallops, mussels, squid, clams, a meaty white fish like cod, or a combination of the above. I like to use a frozen seafood mix from my local supermarket that includes shrimp, scallops, and squid.

TO REFRIGERATE: Store the stew, covered, in the refrigerator for up to two days. To serve, reheat in the microwave or on the stovetop.

TO FREEZE: Let the tomato-broth mixture cool to room temperature, then transfer to a large, resealable plastic bag. Store in the freezer, separate from the frozen seafood, for up to three months. To serve, thaw the soup mixture in the refrigerator overnight, in the microwave, or in a bowl of cold water. Reheat in a stockpot on the stove. Bring to a boil and add the frozen seafood. Let simmer, uncovered, until the seafood is just cooked through, 8 to 10 minutes, and serve hot.

PALEO

DAIRY-FREE

THAI-STYLE CHICKEN SOUP WITH COCONUT MILK

SERVES 4 • PREP TIME: 10 MINUTES • COOK TIME: 30 MINUTES

This recipe is based on a traditional Thai soup that is flavored with lemongrass, but since it can be hard to find in the supermarket, I've substituted strips of lime zest, which work just as well. If you can get lemongrass, feel free to substitute 1 stalk cut into 1-inch pieces. Fish sauce and coconut milk can be found in the international foods aisle of most supermarkets.

Zest and juice of 1 lime

1 pound boneless, skinless chicken breasts (about 3), cut into 2 ½-by-¼-inch strips

3 tablespoons fish sauce

5 cups chicken broth

1 (1-inch) piece fresh ginger, peeled and thickly sliced

½ cup long-grain rice

1 (15-ounce) can coconut milk

2 fresh red chiles or jalapeños, seeded and thinly sliced

3 tablespoons chopped cilantro

Using a vegetable peeler, shave off several strips of zest from the lime and set aside.

In a medium bowl, toss the chicken with the fish sauce and the juice of the lime.

In a stockpot or large saucepan, combine the chicken broth, lime zest, and ginger, and bring to a simmer over medium heat. Add the rice and continue to simmer for about 15 minutes, until the rice is just tender.

Stir in the coconut milk. When the soup begins to simmer again, add the chicken along with the marinade liquid. Cook for about 2 minutes more, until the chicken is cooked through. Stir in the chiles and cilantro. Remove and discard the lime zest and ginger slices. Serve immediately or let cool to room temperature before storing.

GLUTEN-FREE: Use gluten-free broth.

PALEO: Omit the rice.

TO REFRIGERATE: Transfer the soup to a large bowl, cover, and refrigerate for up to three days. To serve, reheat on the stovetop or in the microwave. Serve hot.

TO FREEZE: Portion the soup into single-serving storage containers or resealable plastic bags (either one large one or two small ones), and freeze for up to six months. To serve, thaw in the refrigerator overnight or in the microwave, and reheat either in the microwave or on the stovetop. Serve hot.

DAIRY-FREE

LEMONY CHICKEN AND BROWN RICE SOUP

SERVES 4 TO 6 • PREP TIME: 5 MINUTES • COOK TIME: 50 MINUTES

This soup is wonderfully simple to prepare and uses ingredients you likely have on hand. It's great for using up extra roasted chicken, too. The recipe works perfectly fine with store-bought chicken broth, but it's especially good with homemade broth.

7 cups chicken broth

1 cup brown rice

2 cups diced or shredded cooked chicken

3 large eggs

¼ cup freshly squeezed lemon juice

Kosher salt

In a large saucepan or stockpot, bring the broth to a boil over high heat. Stir in the rice, and lower the heat to medium-low. Simmer, uncovered, for about 45 minutes, until the rice is tender.

Add the chicken and let cook for a few minutes to heat through. Remove the pot from the heat.

In a small bowl, whisk together the eggs and lemon juice.

Add about ½ cup of the hot broth to the egg mixture, and whisk to combine. This helps raise the temperature of the eggs to prevent them from curdling when added to the hot soup.

Stir the egg mixture into the soup. Taste and add salt as needed. Reheat if needed, and serve immediately, or let cool to room temperature before storing.

GLUTEN-FREE: Use gluten-free broth.

TO REFRIGERATE: Store, covered, in the refrigerator for up to two days. Reheat on the stovetop or in the microwave, stirring well if the soup has separated. Serve hot.

TO FREEZE: Freeze in serving-size containers or in a gallon-size resealable plastic bag for up to three months. To serve, thaw in the refrigerator overnight, in the microwave, or on the stovetop. Reheat on the stovetop or in the microwave, stirring well if the soup has separated.

DAIRY-FREE

MINESTRONE SOUP

Minestrone is an Italian vegetable soup. It's also a great "clean-out-the-refrigerator" recipe, where you can use up any odds and ends of vegetables, meats, beans, and pasta, and can be varied it to suit your personal taste. Serve this soup garnished with freshly grated Parmesan cheese and chopped fresh basil. Garlic bread also makes a great accompaniment.

2 tablespoons olive oil

1 onion, diced

4 garlic cloves, minced

2 celery ribs, diced

1 large carrot, diced

⅓ pound green beans, trimmed and cut into ½-inch pieces (about 1½ cups)

2 teaspoons dried oregano

Kosher salt

Freshly ground black pepper

3 (14-ounce) cans crushed tomatoes

6 cups vegetable or chicken broth

1 (15-ounce) can kidney beans, rinsed and drained

1 cup elbow pasta or ditalini

Heat the oil in a large saucepan or stockpot over medium-high heat. Add the onion and garlic, and cook, stirring frequently, until the onions are soft, about 5 minutes. Stir in the celery and carrot, and cook, stirring, until soft, about 5 minutes. Add the green beans and oregano, and season with salt and pepper.

Stir in the crushed tomatoes and broth, and bring to a boil. Lower the heat to medium-low and let the soup simmer for about 10 minutes.

Add the kidney beans and pasta, and cook until the pasta is tender, 10 to 12 minutes more.

GLUTEN-FREE: Use gluten-free broth and pasta (or simply omit pasta).

VEGETARIAN/VEGAN: Use vegetable broth.

TO REFRIGERATE: Store, covered, in the refrigerator for up to three days. Reheat on the stovetop or in the microwave. Serve hot.

TO FREEZE: Freeze in serving-size containers or in a gallon-size resealable plastic bag for up to three months. To serve, thaw in the refrigerator overnight, in the microwave, or on the stovetop. Reheat on the stovetop or in the microwave.

DAIRY-FREE

SLOW COOKER FRENCH ONION SOUP

Classic French onion soup is simple to make but requires long, slow cooking to develop the deep, rich flavors that make it such a winner. The slow cooker provides the perfect solution, making most of the cooking completely hands-off. In fact, once you've made the Slow Cooker Caramelized Onions (page 167), this dish is practically done.

1 batch Slow Cooker Caramelized Onions
  (page 167)
10 cups beef broth
2 tablespoons balsamic vinegar
1 tablespoon minced fresh thyme
Salt
Freshly ground black pepper
1 baguette, sliced into ½-inch-thick rounds
1 cup shredded Gruyère cheese

In a 4- to 6-quart slow cooker, combine the caramelized onions, broth, vinegar, and thyme. Cover and cook on low for 8 hours. Taste and season with salt and pepper, if needed.

If serving the soup immediately, toast the baguette slices on a rimmed baking sheet in the broiler for about 1 minute per side, until golden brown. Place ramekins or other oven-safe serving bowls on a rimmed baking sheet. Fill each bowl with soup, then top with the toasted baguette slices, and sprinkle the cheese over the top, dividing equally among the bowls. Heat under the broiler for about 5 minutes (watch it carefully!), until the cheese bubbles and turns golden brown.

VEGETARIAN: Use vegetable broth.

TIP: If your slow cooker tends to release a lot of steam while cooking, place a clean dishtowel over the top before you put on the lid. This will help prevent the soup from reducing more than you'd like.

TO REFRIGERATE: Let the soup cool to room temperature, then transfer to a bowl and refrigerate, covered, for up to three days. Store the bread and cheese separately in resealable plastic bags. To serve, reheat the soup on the stovetop or in the microwave, and then proceed with serving instructions.

TO FREEZE: Let the soup cool to room temperature, then portion it into single-serving, oven-safe, freezer-safe storage containers, and freeze. If you don't have oven-safe freezer containers, simply use a large, resealable plastic bag. Store the bread and cheese in separate resealable plastic bags. To serve, remove the bread and cheese from the freezer and bring to room temperature on the countertop. Transfer the blocks of frozen soup to oven-safe serving bowls if needed, let thaw, and proceed with serving instructions.

STUFFED CABBAGE SOUP

SERVES 6 • PREP TIME: 5 MINUTES • COOK TIME: 55 MINUTES

Stuffed cabbage is one of my favorite comfort foods, but it's certainly labor intensive. This soup delivers the same comforting flavor with much less work. Serve it with thick slices of crusty bread for dunking.

1 pound extra-lean ground beef

1 onion, diced

3 garlic cloves, minced

½ head cabbage, chopped

1 quart beef broth

3 cups tomato sauce

½ cup uncooked brown rice

3 tablespoons light brown sugar

1 teaspoon kosher salt

½ teaspoon freshly ground black pepper

Juice of 1 lemon

Heat a stockpot or Dutch oven over medium-high heat. Add the beef, onion, and garlic, and cook, stirring and breaking up the meat with a wooden spatula, for about 8 minutes, until the meat is browned and the onions are soft.

Stir in the cabbage, broth, tomato sauce, rice, brown sugar, salt, and pepper. Bring to a boil. Reduce the heat to low, cover, and simmer for about 45 minutes, until the rice is tender.

Remove the pot from the heat, stir in the lemon juice, and serve hot, or let come to room temperature before storing.

GLUTEN-FREE: Use gluten-free broth.

TIP: To keep this recipe healthy, I use extra-lean ground beef and brown rice. You could reduce the fat content even more by substituting ground turkey for the beef.

TO REFRIGERATE: Store, covered, in the refrigerator for up to three days. Reheat on the stovetop or in the microwave, and serve hot.

TO FREEZE: Freeze in serving-size containers or in one gallon-size or two quart-size resealable plastic bags, for up to three months. To serve, thaw in the refrigerator overnight, in the microwave, or on the stovetop. Reheat on the stovetop or in the microwave, and serve hot.

DAIRY-FREE

CHICKEN AND SAUSAGE GUMBO

Gumbo is a flavorful Louisiana-style soup thickened with roux—a mixture of fat and flour that's cooked until it becomes golden brown and nutty. This is a simple version that draws its alluring spice and flavor from peppery Andouille sausage. For a traditional meal, serve it ladled over steamed white rice.

¼ cup vegetable oil

⅓ cup all-purpose flour

1 large onion, diced

1 green bell pepper, diced

4 celery ribs, diced

4 garlic cloves, minced

1 teaspoon kosher salt

½ teaspoon freshly ground black pepper

1 cup canned diced tomatoes or 1 large
    tomato, diced

8 ounces spicy Andouille sausage, cut into 1-inch-
    thick slices

8 ounces diced or shredded cooked chicken

6 cups chicken broth

Heat the oil in the Dutch oven over medium heat for about 5 minutes. Whisk in the flour and cook, continuing to whisk at a constant pace, about 15 minutes, until the mixture turns chestnut brown and gives off a nutty aroma.

Add the onion, bell pepper, and celery, and cook, stirring, over medium heat for about 5 minutes, until the vegetables are soft. Stir in the garlic, salt, and pepper. Stir in the tomato, sausage, and chicken, and cook for 2 minutes more.

Add the broth to the pot and stir well, using a wooden spoon to scrape up any browned bits stuck to the bottom of the pot. Simmer, uncovered, for 25 minutes, until the broth thickens. Serve hot or let cool to room temperature before storing.

TIP: Don't be tempted to skip the roux or try to speed up the process. A well-cooked roux is the key to delicious gumbo, and well worth the time and effort.

TO REFRIGERATE: Store, covered, in the refrigerator for up to three days. Reheat on the stovetop or in the microwave, and serve hot.

TO FREEZE: Freeze in serving-size containers or in one gallon-size or two quart-size resealable plastic bags, for up to three months. To serve, thaw in the refrigerator overnight, in the microwave, or on the stovetop. Reheat on the stovetop or in the microwave, and serve hot.

DAIRY-FREE

SPICY BEEF-AND-BEAN CHILI

SERVES 8 TO 10 • PREP TIME: 10 MINUTES • COOK TIME: 1 HOUR, 10 MINUTES

Chili is one of the best make-ahead dishes because it freezes and reheats so well. This one combines ground beef and beans for a chili as healthy is it flavorful. Serve it with assorted garnishes, including shredded cheese, shredded lettuce, sliced scallions, and avocado.

1 tablespoon olive oil

1 onion, diced

5 garlic cloves, minced

2 pounds ground chuck

3 (15-ounce) cans petite diced tomatoes, with juice

2 (15-ounce) cans pinto beans, rinsed and drained

3 tablespoons tomato paste

3 tablespoons chili powder

2 jalapeños, chopped

1½ teaspoons kosher salt

2 tablespoons minced fresh oregano or 2 teaspoons dried oregano

Heat the olive oil in a stockpot or Dutch oven over medium-high heat. Add the onion and garlic, and cook, stirring frequently, for about 3 minutes, until the onion begins to soften. Add the chuck and cook, stirring and breaking up the meat with a spatula until browned, about 3 minutes more. Drain any excess fat from the pot.

Stir in the tomatoes and their juice, along with the beans, tomato paste, chili powder, jalapeños, salt, and oregano, and bring to a boil. Reduce the heat to low and simmer, uncovered, stirring occasionally, for about 1 hour. Add a bit of water, if needed. Serve hot, or let cool to room temperature before storing.

TIP: For a lighter chili, substitute ground turkey for the ground beef. Even just swapping out half of the beef for a leaner meat will cut the fat content considerably.

TO REFRIGERATE: Store, covered, in the refrigerator for up to three days. Reheat on the stovetop or in the microwave, and serve hot.

TO FREEZE: Freeze in serving-size containers or in one gallon-size or two quart-size resealable plastic bags, for up to three months. To serve, thaw in the refrigerator overnight, in the microwave, or on the stovetop. Reheat on the stovetop or in the microwave, and serve hot.

GLUTEN-FREE

DAIRY-FREE

SLOW COOKER PORK STEW WITH SWEET POTATOES

Sweet potatoes add color and a hint of sweetness to balance out the spicy and savory flavors of the sausage and pork shoulder in this stew. Served with warm corn tortillas and garnished with diced avocado and cilantro, this dish is one of my family's very favorite meals—either straight from the slow cooker or reheated from the freezer.

2 tablespoons cooking oil

1¼ pounds trimmed, boneless pork shoulder, cut into 1½-inch cubes

6 ounces fresh Mexican-style chorizo, removed from casing

¾ pound sweet potatoes, peeled and cut into ½-inch cubes

1 onion, diced

1 garlic clove, minced

1 (28-ounce) can diced tomatoes, drained

2 chipotle peppers in adobo, seeded and minced, plus 4 teaspoons sauce

1 tablespoon minced fresh oregano or 1 teaspoon dried oregano

1 teaspoon kosher salt

In a stockpot or Dutch oven, heat the oil over medium-high heat. Add the pork and chorizo, and cook, stirring frequently, until browned, for about 8 minutes. Transfer the meat to the slow cooker, leaving any excess oil behind.

Add the sweet potatoes, onion, garlic, tomatoes, chipotle peppers and sauce, oregano, and salt. Stir to mix well, then cover and cook on high for 6 to 8 hours, until the meat is very tender. Serve hot, or let cool to room temperature before storing.

TIP: If you can't find chipotles in adobo sauce, substitute ¾ teaspoon ground chipotle peppers or ¼ to ½ teaspoon cayenne plus 1 teaspoon smoked paprika.

TO REFRIGERATE: Store, covered, in the refrigerator for up to three days. Reheat on the stovetop or in the microwave, and serve hot.

TO FREEZE: Freeze in serving-size containers or in one gallon-size or two quart-size resealable plastic bags, for up to three months. To serve, thaw in the refrigerator overnight, in the microwave, or on the stovetop. Reheat on the stovetop or in the microwave, and serve hot.

DAIRY-FREE

VEGETABLE CASSEROLE WITH HERBED RICOTTA (PAGE 81)

chapter five

VEGETARIAN MAINS

LASAGNA WITH RICOTTA, ONIONS, AND CHARD

Creamy ricotta cheese, chard, and onions are layered between tender noodles, Parmesan cheese, and a crunchy breadcrumb topping for a delicious vegetarian entrée. Serve this dish with garlic bread and accompanied by a simple green salad.

2 tablespoons olive oil

2 onions, diced

1½ pounds chard, tough center ribs removed, leaves julienned

2¼ teaspoons salt, divided

1 teaspoon freshly ground black pepper, divided

1 tablespoon chopped fresh sage, divided

½ teaspoon grated nutmeg, divided

3 cups whole milk

½ cup all-purpose flour

¼ cup unsalted butter plus 1 tablespoon unsalted butter, cut into small pieces, divided

2 cups ricotta cheese

1¾ cups grated Parmesan cheese, divided

12 uncooked lasagna noodles

½ cup panko bread crumbs

Preheat the oven to 400°F

Heat the oil in a large skillet over medium-low heat. Add the onions and cook, stirring frequently, for about 5 minutes, until soft. Raise the heat to medium high, and stir in the chard, 1 teaspoon of salt, ½ teaspoon of pepper, 1½ teaspoons of sage, and ¼ teaspoon of nutmeg. Cook, stirring, until the chard is wilted, and no liquid remains in the pan, for 5 to 10 minutes.

In a small saucepan, combine milk, flour, and ¼ cup of the butter and bring to a simmer over medium heat. Lower the heat and cook at a simmer, whisking frequently, until the mixture thickens, about 5 minutes. Stir in ½ cup of the Parmesan, and then remove it from the heat.

In a small bowl, stir the ricotta and ¾ cup of Parmesan, with the remaining 1¼ teaspoons of salt, ½ teaspoon of pepper, 1½ teaspoons of sage, and ¼ teaspoon of nutmeg.

Spoon about ½ cup of the sauce mixture into a 9-by-13-inch baking dish. Use 4 of the noodles to cover the bottom of the dish. Spread one-third of the ricotta mixture over the top of the noodles. Top with half of the chard and another layer of noodles. Repeat, layering half of the remaining sauce mixture and ricotta mixture, the remaining chard, and a layer of noodles. Top with the remaining sauce mixture, the remaining ricotta mixture, and the remaining ½ cup of Parmesan. Sprinkle the breadcrumbs over the top and dot with the remaining tablespoon of butter.

Cover the baking dish with foil, and bake in the preheated oven for 20 minutes. Remove the foil and continue to bake for about 15 minutes more, until the top is golden brown. Serve hot or let cool to room temperature before storing.

TIP: If you have Slow Cooker Caramelized Onions (page 167) prepared, use them in place of the onions in the recipe, skipping the step of sautéing the onions.

TO REFRIGERATE: Cover and refrigerate for up to three days. To serve, cover the lasagna with foil and bake in a 400°F for about 20 minutes, or until heated through.

TO FREEZE: Freeze the lasagna whole, covered in plastic wrap or foil, or cut into individual servings and then wrapped in plastic wrap or foil. To serve, bake from frozen, covered with aluminum foil, in a 400°F oven for about 40 minutes, until heated through.

BLACK BEAN AND ROASTED CHILE BURRITOS

SERVES 12 • PREP TIME: 20 MINUTES • COOK TIME: NONE

These burritos were lifesavers when I was home alone with a newborn baby. This version includes lots of healthy and flavorful ingredients, but you can vary them any way you like. I like to add cabbage to mine to make it a well-rounded meal-in-a-tortilla, but you can leave it out if you prefer. Serve the burritos with your favorite garnishes like salsa, guacamole, or sour cream.

12 whole-wheat burrito-size flour tortillas

3 cups cooked brown rice

3 cups cooked or canned black beans, rinsed and drained

1 (7-ounce) can fire-roasted, diced green chiles

2 cups (about 8 ounces) shredded Monterey Jack, pepper Jack, or sharp Cheddar cheese

2 cups finely shredded cabbage (optional)

Hot sauce (optional)

Lay out several tortillas on your work surface and spoon about ¼ cup of rice down the center of each. Top with about ¼ cup of beans, a spoonful of chilies, about 3 tablespoons of cheese, and a small handful of cabbage, if using. Add hot sauce to taste, if using.

Fold the ends of the burritos in over the filling and then roll the sides around the filling to make classic burrito log shapes.

Repeat until all of the tortillas and filling have been used up.

DAIRY-FREE/VEGAN: Omit the cheese, or substitute dairy-free cheese.

TIP: To keep your burritos from getting soggy, fill them with room-temperature ingredients. Make sure that any ingredients like beans are well drained before you add them to the burrito.

TO REFRIGERATE: Wrap the burritos individually in foil or plastic wrap, and refrigerate for up to three days. To reheat, remove the plastic wrap and wrap the burrito in a damp paper towel. Heat in the microwave on a microwave-safe plate for about 2 minutes, until heated through. You can also reheat the burritos in a lightly oiled skillet on the stovetop.

TO FREEZE: Wrap the burritos individually in foil or plastic wrap and freeze. You can stack the wrapped burritos in the freezer or put them in a large, resealable plastic bag to keep them organized. To reheat, remove the plastic wrap and wrap the burrito in a damp paper towel. Heat in the microwave on a microwave-safe plate for about 4 minutes, turning the burrito over midway, until heated through. You can also reheat the burritos in a lightly oiled skillet on the stovetop, or in foil in a 400°F oven.

VEGETARIAN

BROCCOLI AND CHEESE "MEATBALLS"

SERVES 4 TO 6 • PREP TIME: 15 MINUTES • COOK TIME: 30 MINUTES

These make a great alternative to traditional meatballs. My family loves them served over spaghetti with Marinara Sauce (page 163) or used as a filling for a "meatball" sandwich. They also make a great appetizer served with a creamy salad dressing or garlic aioli for dipping.

1 large head broccoli, cut into florets
¾ cup almond meal
½ cup freshly grated Parmesan cheese
2 garlic cloves, minced
⅛ teaspoon cayenne pepper
½ teaspoon kosher salt
¼ teaspoon freshly ground black pepper
2 large eggs, lightly beaten

Preheat the oven to 350°F.

Line a large, rimmed baking sheet with parchment paper.

Steam the broccoli in a stovetop steamer for about 7 minutes, until tender. Drain and let cool.

In a food processor, pulse the steamed broccoli until finely chopped. Transfer to a large mixing bowl and add the almond meal, Parmesan cheese, garlic, cayenne, salt, and pepper. Stir in the eggs.

Form the mixture into about twenty 1½-inch balls, gently squeezing them to make sure they hold together, and arrange them on the prepared baking sheet. Bake in the preheated oven for about 20 minutes, until golden brown. Serve hot, or let cool to room temperature before storing.

TIP: Form the mixture into patties instead of balls for a tasty take on a veggie burger.

TO REFRIGERATE: Store the balls covered in the refrigerator for up to three days. To reheat, bake in a 350°F oven for about seven minutes on each side.

TO FREEZE: Place the cooked balls into a resealable plastic bag and freeze for up to three months. To reheat, bake in a 350°F oven for about 10 minutes on each side.

VEGETARIAN

VEGAN BLACK BEAN VEGGIE BURGERS

When I'm craving a burger, these really hit the spot, even though they're meat-free. Serve them on burger buns with all the usual fixings—cheese, mayo, mustard, onions, ketchup, pickles, or whatever else you love on a burger.

2 (15-ounce) cans black beans, rinsed and drained
1 cup panko bread crumbs
¼ cup grated onion
2 garlic cloves, finely minced
1 large egg
¾ teaspoon kosher salt
½ teaspoon chili powder
¼ teaspoon freshly ground black pepper
Dash hot sauce (such as Tapatío or Tabasco)
1 tablespoon cooking oil

In a medium mixing bowl, mash the beans with a fork until they're mostly broken up but a few whole beans are still visible. Stir in the bread crumbs, onion, garlic, egg, salt, chili powder, pepper, and hot sauce. Mix to combine well, and then set aside for about 5 minutes.

Form the bean mixture into 4 patties, the size and thickness of a typical hamburger.

To cook and serve immediately, heat the oil in a large skillet over medium-high heat. Cook the freshly made burgers for 3 to 4 minutes per side, until cooked through and browned on the outside. Serve hot.

GLUTEN-FREE: Use gluten-free bread crumbs.

TIP: For extra flavor, use seasoned black beans (drained of excess liquid, but not rinsed). Taste for seasoning before adding salt.

TO REFRIGERATE: Store the burgers covered in the refrigerator for up to three days. To cook, follow the cooking directions above.

TO FREEZE: Freeze the burger patties wrapped in plastic wrap or foil, or with a square of parchment or wax paper between the burgers, in a resealable plastic bag. To cook, heat the oil in a large skillet, and cook the frozen burgers for about seven minutes per side, until thoroughly cooked through and browned on the outside.

VEGAN

DAIRY-FREE

BUTTERNUT SQUASH, SPINACH, AND BLACK BEAN ENCHILADAS

Enchiladas can be frozen either before or after cooking, and are easily reheated (without the extra step of thawing) in the oven. These vegetarian enchiladas are filled with sweet squash, hearty black beans, and spinach for a healthier take on a Mexican classic. I like to use Red Chile Sauce (page 161) for these, but you could just as easily substitute jarred or canned enchilada sauce.

3 cups peeled and cubed butternut squash

1 tablespoon cooking oil

½ teaspoon ground cumin

½ teaspoon kosher salt

½ teaspoon freshly ground black pepper

1 (15-ounce) can black beans, slightly drained

1 (8-ounce) package chopped spinach, thawed, drained, and squeezed to remove excess water

Red Chile Sauce (page 161), divided

10 corn tortillas

1½ cups (about 6 ounces) shredded Monterey Jack or sharp Cheddar cheese

Preheat the oven to 400°F.

Line a 9-by-13-inch pan with aluminum foil.

On a large, rimmed baking sheet, toss the squash with the oil, cumin, salt, and pepper. Spread out into an even layer, and bake in the preheated oven for about 20 minutes, until the squash is tender and beginning to brown.

Transfer the squash to a large bowl, and add the beans, spinach, and a few spoonfuls of Red Chile Sauce. Reduce the oven heat to 350°F.

Wrap the tortillas in a damp towel, and heat in the microwave for 30 seconds.

Coat the bottom of the prepared baking dish with another few spoonfuls of Red Chile Sauce.

Place a tortilla in the baking dish, and fill it with the squash and bean mixture, making a line down the center. Roll the tortilla up around the filling, and place the filled tortilla at one end of the baking dish, seam-side down. Repeat until all the tortillas are filled and rolled. Pour the remaining Red Chile Sauce over the enchiladas. »

VEGETARIAN

73

If you plan to freeze the enchiladas before cooking, skip to the storage instructions. If you plan to bake the enchiladas immediately, sprinkle the cheese over them and bake in the preheated oven for about 20 minutes, until the enchiladas are heated through and the cheese is melted and bubbly. Serve hot, or let cool to room temperature before storing.

DAIRY-FREE/VEGAN: Use soy cheese, or omit the cheese altogether.

TIP: To cut down on prep time, make this dish a casserole. Layer five tortillas on the bottom of the baking dish (tear them into pieces as necessary to fill the dish), cover with filling, and top with the remaining tortillas, sauce, and cheese.

TO REFRIGERATE: Cover cooked enchiladas tightly with aluminum foil, and refrigerate for up to three days. To serve, reheat in a 350°F oven, covered with aluminum foil, for about 25 minutes, until heated through. Individual servings can be reheated in the microwave for two or three minutes on a microwave-safe dish.

TO FREEZE: Freeze uncooked enchiladas, each wrapped tightly with aluminum foil or plastic wrap, for up to three months. Store the shredded cheese in a resealable plastic bag along with the enchiladas. To serve, remove any plastic wrap and place in a 9-by-13-inch baking dish. Sprinkle the cheese over the top, cover with aluminum foil, and bake in a 350°F oven for about 50 minutes, until heated through. (Precooked enchiladas only need to be heated for about 40 minutes.) To brown the top, remove the foil about 15 minutes before the end of cooking or place under a broiler for a few minutes. Serve hot.

SOBA NOODLES AND TOFU IN SPICY PEANUT SAUCE

SERVES 4 • PREP TIME: 15 MINUTES • COOK TIME: 10 MINUTES

This noodle dish is quick to make and loaded with flavor. Use an all-natural peanut butter (one without added sugar) to keep it healthy. Soba noodles, which are made from buckwheat, are naturally gluten-free—but double check the package to make sure no regular wheat has been added.

10 ounces dry soba noodles

⅓ cup smooth peanut butter

⅓ cup warm water

1 tablespoon chopped peeled fresh ginger

1 tablespoon soy sauce

2 tablespoons honey

1 teaspoon crushed red pepper

1 garlic clove, minced

1 carrot, peeled and grated

14 ounces baked tofu, cut into small cubes

Cook the noodles al dente (if serving immediately, cook the noodles fully), according to the package directions. Drain.

In a small bowl, stir together the peanut butter, water, ginger, soy sauce, honey, red pepper, and garlic, until smooth.

In a large mixing bowl, toss together the cooked and drained noodles, peanut sauce, carrot, and tofu. Serve immediately or let cool to room temperature before storing.

TIP: You can substitute any type of noodles you like for this dish. They'll continue to cook during reheating, so be sure to cook them al dente if you're planning to refrigerate or freeze them first and then reheat the dish later.

TO REFRIGERATE: Store, covered, in the refrigerator for up to five days. To serve, heat in a skillet over low heat, adding a bit of water if needed, for about 5 minutes, until heated through.

TO FREEZE: Store in a large, resealable plastic bag, or in four smaller bags, for up to three months. To serve, heat from frozen in a skillet over low heat, adding a bit of water if needed.

VEGETARIAN

GLUTEN-FREE

DAIRY-FREE

SHIITAKE MUSHROOM, CABBAGE, AND EDAMAME POT STICKERS

MAKES 25 TO 30 POT STICKERS • PREP TIME: 30 MINUTES • COOK TIME: 10 MINUTES

Pot stickers are usually served as an appetizer, but these healthy veggie- and edamame-filled dumplings make a satisfying meal all on their own. They can be frozen raw and only take a few minutes to cook from frozen.

2 tablespoons cooking oil, divided

2 ounces shiitake mushrooms, stemmed and finely diced

½ pound shredded cabbage

½ teaspoon kosher salt

4 ounces cooked, shelled edamame

1½ teaspoons minced ginger

1 small garlic clove, minced

2 teaspoons rice wine vinegar

2 teaspoons soy sauce

1 teaspoon sesame oil

25 to 30 round dumpling wrappers

Heat 1 tablespoon of oil in a large skillet over medium-high heat. Add the mushrooms and cook, stirring frequently, until soft and beginning to brown, about 5 minutes. Stir in the cabbage and salt, and cook, stirring occasionally, about 4 minutes more, until the cabbage wilts. Transfer the vegetables to a colander and set over the sink to drain. Let cool for several minutes.

In a large mixing bowl, stir together the edamame, ginger, garlic, vinegar, soy sauce, and sesame oil.

When the mushroom mixture is cool enough to handle, press out as much liquid as possible. Add it to the bowl with the edamame and sauce, and stir to mix well.

Line a large, rimmed baking sheet with parchment paper, and fill a small bowl with water.

To form the dumplings, arrange several wrappers on your work surface and put a tablespoon of filling in the center of each. Dip your finger into the bowl of water and use it to moisten the end of the wrapper all the way around. Lift the sides of the wrapper up and pinch them together over the filling, pleating the wrapper a bit to seal it. Repeat until you have used up all the filling. If you're making the pot stickers in advance, skip to the storage instructions below.

VEGAN

DAIRY-FREE

To cook and serve the pot stickers immediately, heat the remaining tablespoon of oil in a large skillet (choose one that has a tight-fitting lid) over medium-high heat. Place the dumplings in the pan flat-side down, in a single layer. (You'll need to cook the dumplings in batches, but try to fit as many in the skillet as possible without letting them touch.) Cook over medium heat until the bottoms turn golden brown, about 2 minutes. Add ¼ cup of water to the skillet and immediately cover with the lid. Let the dumplings steam for about 5 minutes, until the liquid has been absorbed and the wrappers are tender.

Serve the dumplings hot with a dipping sauce of soy sauce, rice vinegar, and chili paste (or red pepper flakes), if desired.

TIP: If you prefer, you can substitute an equal amount of baked tofu for the edamame. Crumble the tofu before adding it to the sauce mixture.

TO REFRIGERATE: Cover the dumplings with plastic wrap, and refrigerate until ready to cook, for up to two days. To cook, follow the instructions, left.

TO FREEZE: Place the baking sheet filled with dumplings into the freezer, and freeze until solid. Transfer the frozen pot stickers to resealable plastic bags. Follow the cooking instructions, left. If the dumplings are frozen, add a few minutes to the cook time if needed.

HOMEMADE FROZEN PIZZAS

MAKES 4 (8-INCH) PIZZAS • PREP TIME: 20 MINUTES, PLUS UP TO 90 MINUTES
FOR DOUGH TO RISE • COOK TIME: 20 MINUTES

A healthy version of frozen pizza! After a long day, default to this option without a hint of guilt.

2 tablespoons instant yeast
2 cups warm water
2 tablespoons sugar
¼ cup olive oil
2 ½ teaspoons kosher salt
1½ cups all-purpose flour
3 ½ cups whole-wheat flour
2 cups pizza sauce (or Marinara Sauce, page 163)
3 to 4 cups (10 to 12 ounces) shredded cheese

In the bowl of a stand mixer, whisk together the yeast, water, sugar, and oil. Let the mixture sit for about 10 minutes, until it becomes foamy.

Add the salt, all-purpose flour, and whole-wheat flour. Mix/knead using the dough hook for 5 to 7 minutes, until the mixture comes together in a smooth ball. Add up to ¼ cup of water or flour if the dough is either too dry or too wet.

Cover with a clean dishtowel, and set in a warm spot on the countertop for 60 to 90 minutes, until it doubles in size.

Preheat the oven to 400°F.

Divide the dough in half and then in half again, so you have 4 equally sized balls of dough. On a well-floured surface, roll or pat the dough out into circles about ¼ inch thick. Transfer the dough rounds to two large baking sheets. Bake for about 10 minutes, until the outside is dry but not browned. Remove from the oven and let cool completely.

Spread about ½ cup of sauce onto each crust, and then top with the cheese, dividing it equally.

To cook and serve the pizzas immediately, heat the oven to 450°F and bake on a baking sheet or pizza stone for 10 to 12 minutes, until the cheese is melted and bubbling and the crust is golden brown.

TIP: If you don't have a stand mixer, you can mix the dough in a large mixing bowl with a wooden spoon and knead it by hand for about 10 minutes.

TO REFRIGERATE: Tightly wrap the pizzas individually in plastic wrap, and store in the refrigerator for up to three days. To cook and serve the pizzas, bake them in a 450°F oven (on a baking sheet or pizza stone) for 12 to 14 minutes, until the cheese is melted and bubbling and the crust is golden brown.

TO FREEZE: Tightly wrap the pizzas individually in plastic wrap, and store in the freezer for up to three months. To cook and serve the pizzas, bake them from frozen in a 450°F oven (on a baking sheet or pizza stone) for 15 to 17 minutes, until the cheese is melted and bubbling and the crust is golden brown.

VEGETARIAN

PEA-AND-POTATO SAMOSAS

MAKES 24 SAMOSAS • PREP TIME: 25 MINUTES • COOK TIME: 25 MINUTES

Samosas make an irresistible vegetarian entrée. This version is filled with a fairly traditional pea-and-mashed-potato filling, but unlike the traditional deep-fried version, these are baked. I also use phyllo dough in place of homemade pastry dough, because it's easier. Serve these with tamarind or mint chutney for dipping, if you like.

2 tablespoons olive oil, divided
¼ cup finely chopped onion
⅔ cup shredded carrot
⅔ cup fresh or frozen green peas, thawed
1½ teaspoons garam masala
½ teaspoon salt
1 medium potato, boiled and mashed
8 (14-by-9-inch) sheets frozen phyllo
    dough, thawed
Cooking oil spray

Preheat the oven to 350°F.

In a large skillet, heat 1 tablespoon of oil over medium heat. Add the onion and cook, stirring frequently, for 3 minutes, until it begins to soften. Add the carrot and cook for about 2 minutes more. Stir in the peas, garam masala, and salt. Cover the skillet and cook for 2 minutes. Remove from the heat, and stir in the mashed potato.

Working with one sheet of phyllo at a time, while keeping the rest covered with a towel, cut each sheet of phyllo into 3 rectangles measuring 3 by 14 inches. Spray the phyllo lightly with cooking oil spray.

Place 1 tablespoon of the filling at the end of each strip of phyllo. Fold one corner of the strip over the filling to make a triangle. Fold repeatedly in triangles until you reach the end of the strip. As you finish each samosa, place it seam-side down on a baking sheet. Repeat with the remaining filling and sheets of phyllo.

To serve immediately, brush the filled samosas with the remaining 1 tablespoon of oil, and bake in the preheated oven for about 25 minutes, until crisp and lightly browned.

TIP: You can freeze and reheat baked samosas, but they turn out much lighter and crispier if you freeze them unbaked.

TO REFRIGERATE: Cover the unbaked samosas tightly with plastic wrap and refrigerate for up to two days. To serve, brush with the tablespoon of oil and bake in a 350°F oven for 25 minutes, until crisp and lightly browned.

TO FREEZE: Freeze the unbaked samosas on the parchment-lined baking sheet. Once they're frozen solid, transfer them to a resealable bag or freezer container, placing pieces of parchment paper between them to keep them from sticking. They can be frozen for up to three months. To serve, brush the frozen samosas with the tablespoon of oil, and bake in a 350°F oven for about 30 minutes, until crisp and lightly browned.

VEGAN

DAIRY-FREE

CHIPOTLE-TEMPEH TACOS

Tempeh is similar to tofu, but it's made with whole fermented soybeans that are pressed into rectangles. You can usually find it refrigerated alongside the tofu in the supermarket or health-food store. Cooking it in a smoky, spicy lime marinade makes it an ideal vegetarian taco filling. Serve these with Pineapple Salsa (page 162) to add some fruity zing.

FOR THE CHIPOTLE-TEMPEH FILLING
¼ cup freshly squeezed lime juice
¼ cup honey
1 tablespoon soy sauce
1 teaspoon ground chipotle chile
1 teaspoon ground cumin
2 garlic cloves, minced
1 pound tempeh, cut into ½-inch cubes
2 tablespoons cooking oil

FOR SERVING
8 corn tortillas, warmed
2 cups shredded lettuce
Hot or mild salsa

TO MAKE THE FILLING

In a medium bowl, stir together the lime juice, honey, soy sauce, chipotle, cumin, and garlic. Add the tempeh and toss to coat.

Heat the oil in a large skillet over medium heat. Add the tempeh cubes, spreading them out in a single layer and reserving the marinade. Cook for about 10 minutes, turning the tempeh cubes occasionally so that they brown on all sides.

Add the reserved marinade to the skillet and cook until the liquid has evaporated, about 1 minute.

Remove from the heat and serve immediately, or let cool to room temperature before storing.

TO SERVE

Divide the tempeh equally between the tortillas. Top with lettuce and salsa.

GLUTEN-FREE: Use gluten-free tamari instead of soy sauce.

VEGAN: Substitute maple syrup for the honey.

TIP: You can substitute any chili powder you like for the ground chipotle. To maintain the smoky flavor, add a bit of smoked paprika as well.

TO REFRIGERATE: Store the tempeh, covered, in the refrigerator for up to five days. Reheat in a skillet over medium-low heat for about 5 minutes, until heated through, and serve as described above.

TO FREEZE: Transfer the tempeh to a large, resealable plastic bag (or four smaller bags), removing as much air as possible before sealing and freezing flat. Keep frozen for up to three months. To serve, thaw the filling either in the refrigerator overnight or by setting it in a bowl of water for 30 to 60 minutes. Reheat in a skillet over medium-low heat for about 5 minutes, until heated through, and serve as described above.

VEGETARIAN

DAIRY-FREE

VEGETABLE CASSEROLE WITH HERBED RICOTTA

SERVES 6 • PREP TIME: 10 MINUTES • COOK TIME: 55 MINUTES

This hearty vegetable casserole includes all the flavor of lasagna but without any noodles. Perfect to make in the summertime when eggplants and peppers are at their peak, this dish is sure to brighten up a cool fall evening when you pull it out of the freezer a few months later.

2 medium eggplants, cubed

2 red bell peppers (or 1 red and 1 orange or yellow), seeded and cut into 1½-inch pieces

Olive oil spray

Kosher salt

Freshly ground black pepper

14 ounces ricotta cheese

1½ cups freshly grated Parmesan cheese, divided

3 large eggs

2 tablespoons chopped fresh oregano

1 tablespoon chopped fresh basil

3 cups tomato purée or Marinara Sauce (page 163)

Preheat the oven to 425°F.

Line a large, rimmed baking sheet with parchment paper.

Arrange the eggplant and peppers in a single layer on the prepared baking sheet (you may need to do this in two batches or on two baking sheets), and spray them with olive oil. Season with salt and pepper, and bake for 25 minutes.

In a medium bowl, stir together the ricotta, 1 cup of Parmesan cheese, and the eggs, oregano, and basil.

Cover the bottom of a baking dish with a layer of eggplant and peppers. Spoon half of the tomato sauce over the top to cover, then add half of the cheese mixture. Repeat with another layer of eggplant, tomato sauce, and cheese mixture. Sprinkle the remaining ½ cup of Parmesan over the top, and bake in the preheated oven for about 30 minutes, until the topping is bubbling and browned. Serve hot or let cool to room temperature before storing.

TO REFRIGERATE: Cover with plastic wrap and refrigerate for up to three days. To serve, reheat, covered with foil, in a 400°F oven for 15 to 20 minutes, until heated through.

TO FREEZE: Freeze in medium containers or small, resealable plastic bags for up to three months. To serve, thaw in the refrigerator overnight or in the microwave. Then reheat until heated through, either in the microwave or covered with foil in a 400°F oven for 15 to 20 minutes.

VEGETARIAN

GLUTEN-FREE

CREAMY MAC AND CHEESE WITH BROCCOLI AND SILKEN TOFU

SERVES 4 • PREP TIME: 20 MINUTES • COOK TIME: 5 MINUTES
(60 MINUTES IF COOKING FROM FROZEN)

Macaroni and cheese is an indulgent treat—starchy pasta dripping with rich, creamy cheese sauce. Switching out some of the cheese for silken tofu is a brilliant trick that results in a decadent dish. You can substitute another cheese or cheese combination if you like, but since you're using less cheese, be sure to select a cheese with lots of flavor, such as extra-sharp Cheddar.

8 ounces whole-wheat macaroni
2 tablespoons unsalted butter
1 small broccoli head, cut into small florets
2 garlic cloves, minced
1 pound silken tofu
1½ cups shredded extra-sharp Cheddar cheese
1 cup milk
Salt

Cook the macaroni according to the package directions. Drain, return to the cooking pot, and stir in the butter.

While the pasta is cooking, blanch the broccoli in lightly salted boiling water for 3 to 5 minutes, just until tender but still bright green. Drain.

In a blender or food processor, combine the tofu, garlic, cheese, and milk, and process until mostly smooth. (Don't worry if it looks lumpy or grainy.)

Add the sauce and broccoli to the macaroni in the pot, and stir to mix well. Taste and add salt as needed. Let cool to room temperature before storing.

To serve immediately, heat over medium heat, stirring frequently, for about 5 minutes, until the sauce is very creamy and smooth and everything is heated through.

TIP: If you can't find silken tofu, you can easily substitute soft, medium, or firm regular tofu. Though perhaps not as creamy, the result will still be delicious.

TO REFRIGERATE: Refrigerate, covered, for up to three days. To serve, reheat on the stovetop over medium heat, stirring frequently, until the sauce is smooth and creamy and the pasta is heated through. Add a bit of milk, if needed, to keep the sauce from becoming clumpy.

TO FREEZE: Line a baking dish with plastic wrap, and pour the cooled pasta-and-sauce mixture into it. Cover tightly with plastic wrap and freeze until solid. Remove the frozen casserole from the baking dish and add a second layer of wrap to make sure it's well sealed. If you prefer to store it in resealable plastic bags, use either one large bag or four small ones, to keep it frozen for up to three months. To serve, unwrap the casserole and place it in a baking dish. Reheat in the microwave, or heat from frozen in a 400°F oven, covered with foil, for about 1 hour.

VEGETARIAN

THE HEALTHY MAKE-AHEAD COOKBOOK

ROASTED VEGETABLE QUESADILLAS

SERVES 6 • PREP TIME: 10 MINUTES • COOK TIME: 40 MINUTES

I love quesadillas, especially this recipe, which includes robust roasted vegetables and whole wheat tortillas. Wholesome and delicious!

FOR THE ROASTED VEGETABLES

2 medium sweet potatoes (about 1 pound), peeled and cut into 1-inch cubes

1 red bell pepper, seeded and diced

1 red onion, diced

2 tablespoons cooking oil

1 teaspoon kosher salt

1 teaspoon ground cumin

FOR THE QUESADILLAS

6 (8-inch) whole-wheat flour tortillas

2 cups (about 8 ounces) shredded Monterey Jack, pepper Jack, or sharp Cheddar cheese

Cooking oil spray

TO ROAST THE VEGETABLES

Preheat the oven to 450°F.

On a large, rimmed baking sheet, toss together the sweet potatoes, bell pepper, and onion with the oil, salt, and cumin. Spread the vegetables out into an even layer, and roast in the preheated oven for about 30 minutes, stirring once halfway through, until the potatoes are tender and beginning to brown.

TO ASSEMBLE THE QUESADILLAS

Lay three tortillas out on a work surface. Sprinkle about ⅓ cup cheese over each tortilla, and top with roasted vegetables, dividing evenly. Sprinkle the remaining cheese over the vegetables, and top with the remaining three tortillas.

TO COOK THE QUESADILLAS

Spray a large skillet with cooking spray, and heat over high heat. Cook the quesadillas for about 2 minutes per side, until the cheese is melted and the tortilla is lightly browned. To serve immediately, cut each quesadilla in half, cut each half into three wedges, and serve hot. To store, cut each quesadilla in half and let the halves cool to room temperature before storing.

TIP: Use preshredded cheese to cut down on prep time.

TO REFRIGERATE: Wrap each half quesadilla in plastic wrap, and refrigerate for up to three days. To reheat, wrap a quesadilla half in a paper towel, and heat in the microwave on high for 1 to 2 minutes, or heat in a hot skillet sprayed with cooking spray until the cheese is melted.

TO FREEZE: Place the halved quesadillas on a large, rimmed baking sheet, and cover with plastic wrap. Freeze for at least two hours, until frozen solid. Wrap each half quesadilla individually in plastic wrap, and store them in a large, resealable plastic bag in the freezer for up to three months. To serve, wrap the frozen quesadilla in a paper towel and heat on high in the microwave for about 2 minutes, or wrap the quesadilla in foil and heat in a 400°F oven for about 10 minutes.

VEGETARIAN

WHOLE-WHEAT PASTA BAKE WITH MUSHROOMS AND RADICCHIO

SERVES 8 • PREP TIME: 10 MINUTES • COOK TIME: 35 MINUTES

Pasta bakes and casseroles are great to have in the freezer for emergencies. This one combines rich mushrooms, salty cheese, and bitter radicchio with healthy whole-wheat pasta for a simple meal that is complex in flavor. Radicchio is a purple type of chicory, and makes this dish very pretty.

1 pound whole-wheat fusilli pasta

3 tablespoons olive oil

1 pint mushrooms, sliced

1 teaspoon kosher salt, divided

1 medium head radicchio, finely shredded

2 ½ cups half-and-half

½ cup freshly grated Parmesan cheese

1 cup shredded fontina cheese

1 tablespoon chopped fresh sage

Preheat the oven to 400°F.

Cook the pasta al dente according to the package directions.

In a large skillet, heat the olive oil over medium-high heat. Add the mushrooms and ½ teaspoon of salt, and cook, stirring frequently, until softened, about 5 minutes.

In a large mixing bowl, stir together the sautéed mushrooms, radicchio, half-and-half, Parmesan, fontina, sage, and the remaining ½ teaspoon of salt. Add the cooked and drained pasta.

Transfer the mixture to a 9-by-13-inch baking dish. Drizzle the remaining 2 tablespoons of olive oil over the top, and bake in the preheated oven for about 30 minutes, until the cheese is melted and the top is lightly browned in places. Serve hot, or let cool to room temperature before storing.

TIP: If you can't find radicchio, feel free to substitute sliced, fresh fennel bulb or red cabbage instead.

TO REFRIGERATE: Store, covered, in the refrigerator for up to three days. To serve, reheat, covered with aluminum foil, in a 400°F oven for about 20 minutes, or reheat in the microwave.

TO FREEZE: Freeze the casserole whole or divide it into individual freezer containers, and freeze for up to three months. To serve, reheat from frozen, covered with aluminum foil, in a 400°F oven for about 40 minutes, or reheat in the microwave.

VEGETARIAN

BAKED PENNE PUTTANESCA

Puttanesca is a spicy tomato sauce studded with flavorful ingredients like olives and capers. The traditional Italian recipe contains anchovies, but the other ingredients here are so flavorful that you won't miss them if you stick to this vegetarian version. If you do include anchovies, you may want to reduce the salt a bit.

1 tablespoon olive oil

6 garlic cloves, minced

½ teaspoon crushed red pepper flakes

1 teaspoon kosher salt, divided

1 (28-ounce) can crushed tomatoes

3 cups water

12 ounces uncooked whole-wheat penne pasta

½ cup freshly grated Parmesan cheese

¼ cup capers

½ cup pitted and chopped Kalamata olives

1 cup shredded mozzarella cheese

Preheat the oven to 450°F.

In a large skillet, heat the oil over medium-high heat. Add the garlic, red pepper, and ½ teaspoon salt, and cook, stirring, for 1 minute. Stir in the crushed tomatoes, 3 cups of water, the pasta, and the remaining ½ teaspoon of salt, and bring to a boil. Reduce the heat and let simmer for about 10 minutes, until the sauce is thick.

In a 9-by-13-inch baking dish, stir together the sauce, pasta, Parmesan, capers, and olives. Sprinkle the mozzarella evenly over the top, and bake for about 40 minutes, until the pasta is tender and the cheese is melted and browned. Serve hot or let cool to room temperature before storing.

TO REFRIGERATE: Cover and refrigerate for up to three days. To serve, reheat, covered with foil, in a 400°F oven for about 30 minutes, until heated through, or reheat in the microwave.

TO FREEZE: Freeze the casserole whole or divide it into individual freezer containers and freeze for up to three months. To serve, reheat from frozen, covered with aluminum foil, in a 400°F oven for about 40 minutes, or reheat in the microwave.

VEGETARIAN

GRILLED SHRIMP SKEWERS WITH LEMON AND BASIL PESTO (PAGE 89)

chapter six

FISH AND SEAFOOD

SPICY ORANGE BROCCOLI-SHRIMP STIR-FRY

SERVES 4 • PREP TIME: 10 MINUTES, PLUS 1 HOUR TO
DEFROST SHRIMP • COOK TIME: 10 MINUTES

Even a quick stir-fry can be fairly involved, with all the chopping required. But by prepping all the ingredients in advance, you can pull this meal out of the freezer and have it on the table in minutes. This stir-fry combines sweet citrus, spicy red pepper, and plump shrimp for a light, healthy, and delicious meal. Serve it over brown rice or tossed with cooked noodles.

1 tablespoon finely grated orange zest

¼ cup orange juice

¼ cup olive oil

4 garlic cloves, sliced

½ teaspoon kosher salt

¼ to ½ teaspoon crushed red pepper

1½ pounds fresh or frozen peeled and deveined medium shrimp

1 (16-ounce) package frozen broccoli, cauliflower, and carrots

In a small bowl, whisk together the orange zest, orange juice, oil, garlic, salt, and crushed red pepper.

Place the shrimp and vegetables in a 1-gallon resealable plastic bag. Add the orange juice mixture to the bag, toss to mix well, and seal the bag, removing as much air as possible. To freeze or refrigerate, skip to the storage instructions below.

To serve immediately, thaw the vegetables and shrimp by placing the sealed bag in a bowl of cold water for 30 minutes to 1 hour, changing the water once. Heat a large skillet over medium-high heat. Add the shrimp, vegetables, and marinade, and cook, stirring frequently, for 8 to 10 minutes, until the shrimp are cooked through and the vegetables are tender. Serve hot.

TIP: Buy shrimp that are already peeled and deveined to keep prep time to a minimum.

TO REFRIGERATE: The mixture of shrimp, vegetables, and marinade can be stored in the refrigerator overnight. To serve, follow the cooking instructions in step 3.

TO FREEZE: Freeze the shrimp, vegetables, and marinade in the resealable plastic bag for up to one month. To serve, thaw in a bowl of cold water for one hour, changing the water halfway through, or thaw in the refrigerator overnight. Then follow the cooking instructions in step 3.

PALEO

GLUTEN-FREE

DAIRY-FREE

THE HEALTHY MAKE-AHEAD COOKBOOK

GRILLED SHRIMP SKEWERS WITH LEMON AND BASIL PESTO

SERVES 4 • PREP TIME: 10 MINUTES • COOK TIME: 8 MINUTES

Grilling food—either on an outdoor grill or in a grill pan on the stovetop—is a great way to make a flavorful dish in very little time. Serve these skewers with a side of pasta, brown rice, or quinoa, plus a green salad or cooked vegetable.

1½ pounds peeled and deveined shrimp, thawed if frozen

2 lemons, sliced into ¼-inch-thick rounds and then quartered

Kosher salt

Freshly ground black pepper

Fresh Basil Pesto (page 166)

Skewer the shrimp and lemon slices, alternating them and dividing equally among 8 skewers. Season with salt and pepper.

To serve immediately, heat a grill or grill pan to medium-high heat, and grill the skewers for about 3 minutes per side, until the shrimp are cooked through. Brush with the pesto and serve hot.

TO REFRIGERATE: Arrange the filled skewers on a plate, cover tightly with plastic wrap, and refrigerate, along with the Fresh Basil Pesto, for up to 24 hours. To serve, follow instructions, left.

TO FREEZE: Arrange the filled skewers on a parchment-lined baking sheet. Cover with plastic wrap and freeze until solid. Wrap the skewers in the plastic wrap, covering the pointy ends of the skewers, and place in a large, resealable plastic bag along with the Fresh Basil Pesto. Freeze for up to one month. To serve, thaw the shrimp and pesto either in the refrigerator overnight or by placing the bag in a bowl of cold water for up to an hour, changing the water once. Cook following the cooking instructions, left.

GLUTEN-FREE

GINGER SHRIMP CAKES

SERVES 4 TO 6 • PREP TIME: 10 MINUTES, PLUS 30 MINUTES TO
CHILL MIXTURE • COOK TIME: 15 MINUTES

Similar to crab cakes, these succulent shrimp patties get their chewy and satisfying texture from brown rice. I like to serve these with a dollop of garlic aioli and a drizzle of sriracha sauce for a simple but elegant meal. You can also make the patties smaller and serve them as an appetizer.

Cooking oil spray
1½ pounds raw shrimp (thawed if frozen),
    finely chopped
1 cup panko bread crumbs
1½ cups cooked brown rice
1 tablespoon minced fresh ginger
2 garlic cloves, minced
2 tablespoons minced scallions
2½ tablespoons soy sauce
3 large eggs, lightly beaten

Preheat the oven to 400°F.

Spray a baking sheet with cooking oil spray.

In a large mixing bowl, mix together the shrimp, bread crumbs, rice, ginger, garlic, scallions, soy sauce, and eggs. Refrigerate for 30 minutes. Form into 8 patties and arrange the patties on the prepared baking sheet.

Spritz the patties with cooking spray, and bake for about 14 minutes, until the shrimp is opaque and the patties are cooked through. Serve hot or let cool to room temperature before storing.

TIP: If you prefer, you can substitute scallops, crab, or other shellfish, or even a meaty white fish like cod, for the shrimp.

TO REFRIGERATE: Cover the patties with plastic wrap, and refrigerate for up to 24 hours. To serve, follow the instructions above.

TO FREEZE: Place the patties in the freezer on the baking sheet, and freeze until solid, at least four hours. Transfer the frozen patties to a resealable plastic bag, placing squares of parchment in between the patties to prevent sticking, and freeze for up to three months. To serve, reheat from frozen on a baking sheet in a 400°F oven for 10 to 15 minutes.

DAIRY-FREE

SALSA VERDE SHRIMP ENCHILADA BAKE

SERVES 4 • PREP TIME: 15 MINUTES • COOK TIME: 30 MINUTES

These flavorful enchiladas include a tangy green sauce and a filling of plump, juicy shrimp. Serve these with all the trimmings: a dollop of low-fat sour cream, guacamole, chopped cilantro, and/or salsa.

2 (28-ounce) cans tomatillos, drained

1 (7-ounce) can diced fire-roasted green chiles

2 garlic cloves

2 cups packed chopped cilantro

1 pound peeled and deveined shrimp, thawed if frozen, and chopped

1 teaspoon ground cumin

1 teaspoon chili powder

¼ teaspoon kosher salt

½ cup low-fat sour cream

10 corn tortillas

8 ounces shredded Monterey Jack or Cheddar cheese

Preheat the oven to 350°F. Line a baking dish with aluminum foil for easy removal of enchiladas for storage, or use a disposable aluminum baking dish.

To make the salsa verde, combine the tomatillos, chiles, garlic, and cilantro in a blender or food processor, and process to a smooth purée.

In a large bowl, stir together ¼ cup of the salsa verde with the shrimp, cumin, chili powder, salt, and sour cream.

Wrap the tortillas in a damp towel and heat in the microwave for 30 seconds to soften them. Spread about ⅔ cup of the salsa verde in the bottom of a 9-by-13-inch baking dish. Place about ¼ cup of the filling into a tortilla. Roll up the tortilla around the filling and place it seam-side down in the baking dish. Repeat with the remaining tortillas and filling.

Spoon the remaining salsa verde over the enchiladas, covering them completely. If making ahead, skip to the storing instructions on the next page. »

GLUTEN-FREE

To serve immediately, sprinkle the cheese over the top, cover the pan with aluminum foil, and bake for 20 minutes. Remove the foil and continue baking until the cheese is melted and begins to brown, about 10 minutes more.

TIP: To cut down on prep time, substitute a preshredded Mexican cheese blend for the Monterey Jack or Cheddar.

TO REFRIGERATE: Cover the pan of enchiladas tightly with aluminum foil or plastic wrap, and refrigerate, with the shredded cheese in a separate resealable plastic bag, for up to two days. To serve, follow the instructions above, adding about 5 minutes to the initial cooking time.

TO FREEZE: If you lined the baking dish with foil, use the foil to lift the frozen enchiladas from the baking dish, wrap them tightly, and store them in the freezer for up to three months. Store the shredded cheese along with the enchiladas in a resealable plastic bag. To serve, place the frozen enchiladas in a baking dish, sprinkle the cheese over the top, cover with aluminum foil, and bake in a 350°F oven for about 40 minutes, until heated through. Remove the foil and bake for about 10 minutes more, until the cheese is melted and beginning to brown.

FISH TACOS WITH PINEAPPLE SALSA

SERVES 4 TO 6 • PREP TIME: 5 MINUTES • COOK TIME: 10 MINUTES

Most fish tacos include fried fish, but for this lighter version, the fish is seasoned with Mexican spices and pan-seared. Serve these topped with shredded lettuce or cabbage (for some crunch), sliced avocado or guacamole, and even sour cream, if you like.

1 teaspoon chili powder

1 teaspoon ground cumin

1 teaspoon kosher salt

1½ pounds firm white fish fillets such as cod, mahi mahi, or halibut

12 corn tortillas

2 tablespoons cooking oil

Shredded cabbage (optional)

Pineapple Salsa (page 162)

In a small bowl, combine the chili powder, cumin, and salt. Sprinkle the spice mixture on both sides of the fish fillets. To store, skip to the instructions on storing below.

To serve immediately, preheat the oven to 400°F.

Wrap the tortillas in aluminum foil and heat in the oven for about 10 minutes.

Meanwhile, heat the oil in a large skillet over medium heat. Cook the fish for about 4 minutes per side, until cooked through and lightly browned. Cut the fish into 2-inch strips and divide them among the warmed tortillas. Top with shredded cabbage (if using) and salsa, and serve immediately.

TO REFRIGERATE: Wrap the seasoned fish fillets tightly in plastic wrap, and store in the refrigerator, along with the pineapple salsa, tortillas, and toppings, for up to 24 hours. To serve, follow the instructions above.

TO FREEZE: Wrap each seasoned fish fillet tightly in plastic wrap, and store in a large, resealable plastic bag along with the tortillas and salsa in separate, resealable plastic bags. To serve, thaw in the refrigerator overnight, or by placing the bag with the fish and salsa in a bowl of water for about one hour, changing the water once. Follow the cooking instructions above.

GLUTEN-FREE

DAIRY-FREE

FENNEL AND TOMATO BAKED HALIBUT FILLETS

SERVES 4 TO 6 • PREP TIME: 10 MINUTES • COOK TIME: 40 MINUTES

Fish baked in a flavorful sauce is one of the best quick-fix dinners, and it's even better if you have all the elements ready to go ahead of time. I like to use meaty halibut for this dish, but other fish like cod, mahi mahi, or even salmon work equally well.

1 tablespoon olive oil

1 small fennel bulb, trimmed and diced

1 small onion, diced

2 garlic cloves, minced

1 (14.5-ounce) can diced tomatoes, with juice

⅓ cup red wine

¼ teaspoon crushed red pepper

Kosher salt

Freshly ground black pepper

1½ pounds halibut fillets

Heat the olive oil in a large skillet over medium-high heat. Add the fennel, onion, and garlic, and cook, stirring frequently, for about 5 minutes, until soft. Add the tomatoes along with their juice, as well as the wine, crushed red pepper, salt, and pepper. Bring to a boil, then reduce the heat to medium-low and simmer the sauce, uncovered, for about 20 minutes.

If planning to store the dish, cool the sauce completely and skip ahead to the storage instructions.

To serve immediately, preheat the oven to 400°F. Arrange the fish in a large baking dish. Pour the sauce over the top and transfer to the oven. Bake for 15 to 20 minutes, until the fish is cooked through. Serve hot.

TO REFRIGERATE: Store the sauce, covered, in the refrigerator for up to a week. Store the fish, wrapped in plastic wrap, in the refrigerator for up to two days. To serve, follow the instructions above.

TO FREEZE: Transfer the sauce to a large, resealable plastic bag and remove most of the air to freeze flat. Wrap the fish fillets individually in plastic wrap. Store both the sauce and fish in an extra-large, resealable plastic bag. The fish and sauce can be frozen for up to three months. To serve, thaw the fish and sauce overnight in the refrigerator or in a bowl of cold water for up to an hour, changing the water once. Cook according to the instructions above, adding a few minutes to the cooking time if needed.

GLUTEN-FREE

DAIRY-FREE

BAKED COD FILLETS WITH LEMON-HERB BREAD CRUMBS

Fish with a crunchy topping of bread crumbs and herbs makes for a delightfully fresh-tasting meal that you'd never suspect came out of the freezer. I like to serve this fish with steamed green beans and baked or mashed sweet potatoes.

½ cup panko bread crumbs

1 tablespoon chopped fresh chives

1 tablespoon chopped fresh parsley

1 garlic clove, minced

Zest of 1 lemon

½ teaspoon paprika

½ teaspoon kosher salt, plus additional for seasoning the fish

2 tablespoons unsalted butter

1½ pounds cod fillets

In a small bowl, stir together the bread crumbs, chives, parsley, garlic, lemon zest, paprika, and ½ teaspoon salt. If making ahead, skip to the storage instructions below.

To serve immediately, preheat the oven to 400°F. Line a large, rimmed baking sheet with parchment paper.

Melt the butter. Arrange the fish fillets on the prepared baking sheet, season with salt, and brush each fillet with melted butter. Sprinkle the bread crumb mixture over the top of the fish fillets, dividing it equally among the fillets. Bake in the preheated oven for about 10 minutes, until the fish is cooked through and flakes easily. Serve hot.

DAIRY-FREE: Substitute olive oil for butter.

GLUTEN-FREE: Substitute gluten-free bread crumbs.

TO REFRIGERATE: Wrap the fish tightly in plastic wrap and store for up to 24 hours. Store the bread crumb mixture and butter separately. To serve, follow the instructions, left.

TO FREEZE: Transfer the bread-crumb mixture to a small, resealable plastic bag. Wrap the butter and each of the fish fillets separately in plastic wrap. Store the wrapped fish fillets, butter, and bread crumbs together in one large, resealable plastic bag for up to three months. To serve, thaw the fish in the refrigerator overnight or in a bowl of cold water for up to an hour, changing the water once. Then follow the cooking instructions, left.

GINGER-SOY GLAZED SALMON

This recipe is deceptively simple. The marinade for the salmon fillets contains only a few simple ingredients, but the flavor is spectacular. If you prefer your food spicy, kick it up a notch and add a spoonful of chili paste to the marinade. Serve this dish with steamed broccoli and brown rice.

⅓ cup soy sauce

¼ cup brown sugar

2 garlic gloves, minced

1 tablespoon minced fresh ginger

1½ pounds skinless salmon fillets

In a small bowl, combine the soy sauce, sugar, garlic, and ginger, and mix well.

Put the salmon fillets in a large, resealable plastic bag, and pour the soy sauce mixture over it. Seal the bag and shake it a bit to make sure the salmon is well coated. If making ahead, skip to the storage instructions below.

To serve immediately, refrigerate the salmon in the marinade for at least an hour.

Preheat the oven to 425°F.

Transfer the salmon to a baking dish, arrange the fillets in a single layer, and pour the marinade over the top. Bake in the preheated oven for 12 to 15 minutes, until the fish flakes easily with a fork. Serve hot.

GLUTEN-FREE: Use gluten-free tamari instead of soy sauce.

TIP: If you're using wild-caught salmon, check it after it has been in the oven for 10 minutes. It's leaner than farmed salmon, so it cooks more quickly and can dry out if overcooked.

TO REFRIGERATE: Store the salmon in the bag with the marinade in the refrigerator for up to 24 hours. To serve, follow the instructions in steps 4 and 5 above.

TO FREEZE: Freeze the salmon and marinade in the bag for up to three months. To serve, thaw the fish either in the refrigerator overnight or in a bowl of water for up to an hour, changing the water once. Once thawed, cook according to the instructions above.

DAIRY-FREE

CRISPY BAKED FISH STICKS

SERVES 8 • PREP TIME: 10 MINUTES • COOK TIME: 20 MINUTES

Fish sticks are always a family favorite. This version is healthier than what you normally find at the supermarket because it's oven-baked instead of fried, and also contains a mix of whole-wheat and panko bread crumbs. I keep a bag of these in the freezer at all times. Serve them with Tangy Coleslaw (page 152), and ketchup or tartar sauce for dipping.

1¼ cups whole-wheat bread crumbs
1¼ cups panko bread crumbs
⅓ cup olive oil
¾ teaspoon kosher salt
½ teaspoon pepper
3 large eggs
2½ pounds cod or flounder fillets, cut crosswise into ¾-inch-wide strips

Preheat the oven to 450°F.

On a large rimmed baking sheet, combine the bread crumbs, oil, salt, and pepper. Toss together. Spread the crumbs out into an even layer on the baking sheet and toast in the preheated oven for about 5 minutes, tossing once midway, until the crumbs begin to turn golden. Transfer the toasted crumbs to a shallow bowl. Wipe off the baking sheet and line it with parchment paper. Leave the oven on if you plan to bake the fish sticks right away. Otherwise turn it off.

Crack the eggs into a separate shallow bowl and beat lightly.

Dip the fish strips into the eggs, let excess drip back into the bowl, and then dredge in the bread crumbs, pressing to help the crumbs stick to the fish. Arrange the coated fish sticks in a single layer on the prepared baking sheet. Repeat until all of the fish is coated with crumbs. If you're making ahead, skip to the storage instructions below.

To serve immediately, bake the fish sticks in the preheated oven for 12 to 15 minutes, until they are crisp and golden brown on the outside and cooked through. Serve hot.

TIP: You can use any type of meaty fish you like for these, but look for fillets on the thicker side for the best fish-to-coating ratio.

TO REFRIGERATE: Cover the fish sticks with plastic wrap and store in the refrigerator for up to two days. To serve, follow the cooking instructions above.

TO FREEZE: Cover the fish sticks with plastic wrap and freeze on the baking sheet until solid. Transfer the frozen fish sticks to a large, resealable plastic bag, and freeze for up to three months. To serve, cook them from frozen in a single layer on a parchment-lined baking sheet in a 450°F oven for about 20 minutes, until crisp, golden brown, and cooked through.

DAIRY-FREE

CHICKEN BREAST IN CHIMICHURRI SAUCE (PAGE 116)

POULTRY

HERB-ROASTED CHICKEN

A simple roast chicken makes a lovely Sunday family meal, especially this one with its delicate herb seasoning. It also makes great leftovers that you can use to create all kinds of other dishes, like Chicken Pot Pies with Whole-Wheat Crust (page 105) or Chicken-and-Spinach Enchiladas in Red Chile Sauce (page 114).

4 tablespoons unsalted butter, at room temperature

5 garlic cloves, divided (3 minced, 2 halved)

4 sprigs fresh rosemary, divided (3 finely chopped, 1 left whole)

1 teaspoon kosher salt, plus extra for seasoning the chicken

½ teaspoon freshly ground black pepper, plus extra for seasoning the chicken

2 lemons (zest, and then juice)

2 large onions, sliced

1 whole chicken (about 4 pounds), giblets removed, rinsed and patted dry

Preheat the oven to 475°F.

In a small bowl, stir together the butter, minced garlic, chopped rosemary, salt, pepper, and the zest of both lemons.

Spread the onions in an even layer in the bottom of a large Dutch oven or roasting pan.

Season the inside of the chicken cavity generously with salt and pepper.

Halve and juice the zested lemons. Set both the juice and the rinds aside.

With your hands, slather the butter mixture all over the skin of the chicken and also under the skin of the breast. Place the lemon rinds, halved garlic cloves, and the whole rosemary sprig inside the cavity. Place the chicken in the Dutch oven or roasting pan on top of the onions, and drizzle the reserved lemon juice over the top.

Roast the chicken, uncovered, in the preheated oven for 15 minutes, then reduce heat to 350°F and cook for 50 to 60 minutes longer, basting once or twice if desired.

PALEO: Use ghee instead of butter.

TIP: To cook the chicken in a slow cooker, follow the instructions as written through step 6, placing the onions and chicken in the insert of your slow cooker. Cover and cook for about 9 hours on low or 5 hours on high. The chicken will be extremely tender, but you won't get a crisp skin.

TO REFRIGERATE: The cooked chicken can be refrigerated for up to three days. You can either refrigerate the meat on the bone or pull the meat off the bone first. If you leave the meat on the bone, you might want to cut the chicken into pieces (breast, thigh, etc.) for easier reheating. To serve, use the pulled meat in dishes calling for cooked chicken, like tacos, enchiladas, or soups. You could also heat on-the-bone pieces in a foil-covered baking dish in a 350°F oven for about 15 minutes, or in the microwave.

TO FREEZE: Pull the meat off the bone, discarding the skin. Place the meat in a large, resealable plastic bag or a few smaller bags, and remove as much air as possible. Freeze for up to three months. To serve, thaw the chicken overnight in the refrigerator and use it in dishes that call for cooked chicken, such as enchiladas, chicken pot pies, or soup.

CHICKEN ROASTED WITH GARLIC, LEMON, AND ROOT VEGETABLES

SERVES 4 • PREP TIME: 10 MINUTES, PLUS 30 MINUTES TO MARINATE • COOK TIME: 40 MINUTES

This one-pot roast-chicken-and-veggie dinner is easy to toss together and even easier to cook. Feel free to mix up the combination of vegetables. I sometimes add green beans, butternut squash, or other root vegetables like turnips or parsnips.

¼ cup olive oil

Juice of 1 lemon

4 garlic cloves, minced

1 teaspoon kosher salt

½ teaspoon freshly ground black pepper

1 teaspoon dried oregano

2 medium red potatoes, diced

1 medium sweet potato, diced

3 large carrots, sliced

4 boneless, skinless chicken breasts (about
    2 pounds)

In a large bowl, combine the oil, lemon juice, garlic, salt, pepper, and oregano. Add the potatoes, sweet potatoes, carrots, and chicken to the marinade, and toss to coat. (If you're freezing the meal, skip ahead to the storage instructions.)

If preparing immediately, let the meat and vegetables marinate in the refrigerator for at least 30 minutes.

Preheat the oven to 425°F.

Transfer the chicken, vegetables, and marinade to an 8-by-8-inch baking dish, arranging the chicken breasts on top of the vegetables. Roast in the preheated oven, uncovered, for about 40 minutes, until the chicken is cooked through and the vegetables are tender. Serve hot.

PALEO: Omit the red potatoes.

TIP: If the chicken is cooked through by the end of the roasting time but the vegetables aren't completely tender, transfer the chicken breasts to a cutting board and tent with foil, then return the baking dish containing the vegetables to the oven to continue roasting for another 10 minutes or so.

TO REFRIGERATE: The cooked dish can be refrigerated, covered, for up to three days. To serve, reheat, covered with aluminum foil, in a 375°F oven until heated through, about 15 minutes, or reheat in the microwave.

TO FREEZE: After completing step 1 above, transfer the chicken, vegetables, and marinade to a large, resealable plastic bag and freeze flat. The dish can be stored in the freezer for up to three months. To serve, thaw in the refrigerator overnight, then follow the cooking instructions above.

GLUTEN-FREE

DAIRY-FREE

PAN-ROASTED CHICKEN WITH OLIVES AND GRAPES

SERVES 4 TO 6 • PREP TIME: 10 MINUTES • COOK TIME: 25 MINUTES

Olives and grapes create a pleasing contrast between sweet and salty. Oven-roasting chicken thighs keeps them moist and infuses them with rich flavor. Serve this dish over cooked couscous or brown rice, spooning the sauce over the top so that it soaks into the grains.

8 skin-on, bone-in chicken thighs (about 3 pounds)

Kosher salt

Freshly ground black pepper

2 tablespoons cooking oil

3 garlic cloves, minced

1 cup pitted Kalamata olives

2 sprigs fresh oregano

1 cup dry white wine

½ cup water

2 cups seedless grapes (red, green, or a combination), divided

2 tablespoons unsalted butter

Season the chicken generously with salt and pepper. Heat the oil in a large, oven-safe skillet over medium-high heat. When the oil begins to shimmer, add the chicken, skin-side down. (You may need to cook the chicken in two batches.) Cook for about 4 minutes, until the skin is golden brown. Turn the chicken pieces over and cook for another 3 to 4 minutes, until the second side is browned. Transfer the browned chicken to a plate.

Lower the heat to medium and add the garlic, olives, oregano, wine, water, and 1 cup of grapes. Cook, stirring, for about 7 minutes, until the liquid has been reduced by half. Swirl in the butter.

Return the chicken and any accumulated juices to the skillet, arranging the chicken skin-side up. Add the remaining cup of grapes, and continue to cook for 8 minutes more. If you're freezing or refrigerating, skip ahead to the storage instructions.

To serve, preheat the broiler to high and transfer the skillet to the broiler. Broil for 2 to 3 minutes, until the skin is crisp. Serve immediately.

TO REFRIGERATE: Cook the dish according to the instructions at left, then store, covered, in the refrigerator for up to three days. To serve, reheat in a covered baking dish in a 350°F oven for about 15 minutes, then broil according to the instructions above.

TO FREEZE: Cook the dish according to instructions at left, then let cool to room temperature. Transfer the chicken, along with the sauce, olives, and grapes, to one or two resealable plastic bags. Remove as much air as possible and freeze flat. To serve, thaw in the refrigerator overnight or in the microwave. Then reheat, covered, in a 350°F oven for 15 to 20 minutes, or in the microwave. Follow the instructions above for the final broil.

DAIRY-FREE

CAJUN-SPICED TURKEY MINI MEAT LOAVES

MAKES 12 MINI LOAVES • PREP TIME: 10 MINUTES • COOK TIME: 45 MINUTES

These muffin tin meat loaves are a convenient way to prepare and store meat loaf in individual servings. They're also great for packing in a lunch box, or you can slice them for sandwiches. Add more or less spice, according to your personal preference.

Cooking oil spray
2 pounds ground turkey
1 onion, finely diced
1 cup old-fashioned rolled oats
¼ cup tomato paste
4 garlic cloves, minced
1½ tablespoons Cajun seasoning, such as
    Tony Chachere's
1 large egg, lightly beaten
½ cup spicy mustard

Preheat the oven to 350°F.

Spray a muffin tin with cooking oil spray.

In a large bowl, combine the turkey, onion, oats, tomato paste, garlic, Cajun seasoning, and egg. Mix well.

Transfer the meat mixture to the muffin tin, dividing equally between the wells. Spread the mustard over the tops. If you plan to freeze the meat loaves, skip to the freezing instructions.

To bake, cover the muffin tin with aluminum foil and bake in the preheated oven for 15 minutes. Remove the foil and continue to bake, uncovered, for about 30 minutes more, until the meat is cooked through. Let rest for 5 minutes before serving.

GLUTEN-FREE: Use gluten-free oats.

TIP: You can also make this recipe as one large meat loaf instead of individual loaves. See Classic Meat Loaf (page 126) for cooking times.

TO REFRIGERATE: Once the meat loaves are at room temperature, cover and store in the refrigerator for up to three days. To serve, reheat in the microwave or wrapped in foil in a 350°F oven for 15 to 20 minutes.

TO FREEZE: Cover the muffin tin containing the uncooked meat loaves and freeze at least 2 hours, until frozen solid. Transfer the frozen meat loaves to a large, resealable plastic bag, and store in the freezer for up to three months. To serve, cook the frozen meat loaves, covered with foil, in a muffin tin in a 350°F oven for 45 minutes, then uncover and cook for about 20 minutes more.

DAIRY-FREE

CHICKEN POT PIES WITH WHOLE-WHEAT CRUST

MAKES 6 INDIVIDUAL POT PIES • PREP TIME: 10 MINUTES • COOK TIME: 1 HOUR, 10 MINUTES

Freshly baked, individual chicken pot pies are the perfect weeknight meal—especially these, which you can make in a flash! For this recipe you'll need six 8-ounce ramekins or disposable foil containers. I use store-bought whole-wheat pie dough when I'm pressed for time, but homemade is even better.

4 tablespoons (½ stick) unsalted butter

1 onion, diced

¾ cup all-purpose flour

5 cups chicken broth

2 cups carrots, diced

¼ cup half-and-half

1 large russet potato, diced

1 (10-ounce) package frozen peas (2 cups)

3 cups chopped, cooked chicken

1 teaspoon kosher salt

½ teaspoon freshly ground black pepper

1 (16-ounce) package whole-wheat pie dough, or homemade pie dough

Preheat the oven to 350°F.

Melt the butter in a large saucepan over medium-high heat. Add the onion and cook, stirring frequently, until soft, about 5 minutes. Reduce the heat to low, stir in the flour, and continue to cook, stirring, for 2 minutes. Add the broth and carrots and simmer for 3 minutes more. Add the half-and-half, potatoes, peas, chicken, salt, and pepper and stir to mix. Remove the pan from the heat.

Roll the pie dough out ¼ inch thick. Cut out crusts for the pies, gauging the size by using one of the ramekins or foil containers in which you plan to cook the pies. Allow for the fact that the crusts will overhang the sides of the containers by about ¾ inch.

Place the containers on a large, rimmed baking sheet, and fill each all the way to the top with the chicken mixture. Lay a pie crust on top of each filled container, and press it around the edge to seal. Poke a few holes in the crust with a fork or the tip of a sharp knife. If you're planning to freeze the pies, skip ahead to the freezing instructions.

To bake, preheat the oven to 375°F. Place the baking sheet containing the pies in the preheated oven and bake for 1 hour. Serve hot. »

GLUTEN-FREE: Use gluten-free pie crust and broth.

TIP: If the crust begins to brown too much before the filling is thoroughly heated, cover the pies with aluminum foil for the remainder of the baking time.

TO REFRIGERATE: The baked pies can be refrigerated for up to three days. To serve, reheat in a 375°F oven for 20 to 30 minutes, until heated through.

TO FREEZE: Cover each of the unbaked pies with plastic wrap or aluminum foil, and place the baking sheet containing the pies in the freezer. Freeze until solid, at least two hours. Once frozen, the pies can be stacked in the freezer and stored for up to three months. To serve, thaw in the refrigerator overnight and bake according to step 5 above, or bake from frozen in a 375°F oven for about 1½ hours, or until internal temperature reaches at least 140°F.

HOMEMADE CRUNCHY CHICKEN TENDERS

SERVES 4 • PREP TIME: 10 MINUTES • COOK TIME: 40 MINUTES

I love to keep these chicken tenders in my freezer and often serve them as a simple entrée with dipping sauce and veggies on the side. They're also great for topping a Cobb salad, or douse them with tomato sauce and cheese then tuck into a roll for a quick chicken Parmesan sandwich.

1 cup all-purpose or whole-wheat flour

1 teaspoon kosher salt

1 teaspoon freshly ground black pepper

1 teaspoon garlic powder

1 teaspoon paprika

2 large eggs

1 cup panko bread crumbs

1½ pounds chicken tenders

Line a large, rimmed baking sheet with parchment paper.

In a shallow bowl, combine the flour, salt, pepper, garlic powder, and paprika, and stir to mix.

In a separate shallow bowl, whisk the eggs.

Place the bread crumbs in a third shallow bowl.

Dunk the chicken tenders one at a time first into the flour mixture, then into the egg, allowing the excess to drip back into the bowl, and finally into the bread crumbs to coat completely. Arrange the coated strips on the prepared baking sheet. If freezing the chicken tenders, skip ahead to the storage instructions.

To bake, preheat the oven to 350°F. Bake the chicken tenders for about 25 minutes, until golden brown and crisp on the outside and cooked through. Serve hot.

TO REFRIGERATE: The coated chicken tenders can be covered and refrigerated for up to an hour. To serve, follow the baking instructions above.

TO FREEZE: Transfer the baking sheet containing the coated but unbaked chicken tenders to the freezer. Freeze until solid, at least two hours. Transfer the chicken tenders to a large, resealable plastic bag and store frozen for up to three months. To serve, preheat the oven to 350°F and bake the chicken tenders on a parchment-lined baking sheet for about 40 minutes, until golden brown and crisp on the outside and cooked through on the inside.

DAIRY-FREE

OVEN-FRIED CHICKEN

Oven-baking instead of deep-frying is a faster, neater method of cooking "fried" chicken. It also produces a lower-fat dish. Using cornflake crumbs to coat the chicken makes it extra crispy. Enjoy this dish hot out of the oven or at room temperature for a take-along meal. This recipe is also perfect for picnics.

Cooking oil for preparing the baking sheet

2 large eggs

¼ cup milk

1 tablespoon hot sauce, or more for seasoning

2 teaspoons salt

1 teaspoon garlic powder

1 teaspoon paprika

½ teaspoon ground black pepper

2½ cups crushed cornflake cereal

3½ pounds skinless, bone-in chicken thighs and drumsticks, rinsed and patted dry

Lightly oil a large, rimmed baking sheet.

In a shallow bowl, whisk together the eggs, milk, hot sauce, salt, garlic powder, paprika, and pepper. Place the crushed cornflakes in a separate shallow bowl.

Dip the chicken, one piece at a time, into the egg mixture and then into the cornflakes, pressing to make the crumbs stick. Arrange the coated chicken pieces on the prepared baking sheet. If freezing, skip ahead to the storage instructions.

To cook, preheat the oven to 350°F. Bake the chicken for 50 to 60 minutes, until the coating is golden brown and crisp and the chicken is cooked through. Serve hot or at room temperature.

TIP: If you prefer chicken breasts to thighs and drumsticks, use boneless, skinless breasts, cut them in half, and reduce the baking time to 35 to 40 minutes.

TO REFRIGERATE: The coated, uncooked chicken can be kept in the refrigerator, uncovered, for up to three hours. To cook, follow the instructions above.

TO FREEZE: Place the baking sheet of chicken pieces in the freezer and freeze at least two hours, until frozen solid. Wrap the chicken pieces individually in plastic wrap, and store in a large, resealable plastic bag for up to three months. To cook, follow the directions above, adding about 20 minutes to the cooking time.

GLUTEN-FREE

TANDOORI-STYLE CHICKEN

A *tandoor* is a clay oven, ubiquitous in much Indian cooking. While few home cooks have access to this specialized piece of equipment, the namesake chicken recipe here duplicates much of the flavor and texture of this classic through the use of the traditional Indian technique of marinating chicken in spiced yogurt. This makes it particularly tender and helps the meat absorb the intense, fragrant flavors of tangy lemon juice and garam masala, a complex Indian spice mixture including cinnamon, cloves, cardamom, and other spices. You can find garam masala in the spice section of most supermarkets.

1½ cups plain yogurt
2 tablespoons cooking oil
1½ tablespoons lemon juice
1 (1-inch) piece fresh ginger, peeled and chopped
4 garlic cloves, minced
1 tablespoon garam masala
2 teaspoons paprika
1 teaspoon kosher salt
½ teaspoon freshly ground black pepper
8 chicken thighs or drumsticks, or a combination

In a food processor, combine the yogurt, oil, lemon juice, ginger, garlic, garam masala, paprika, salt, and pepper.

Place the chicken in a large, resealable plastic bag and pour the yogurt mixture over the chicken. Seal the bag and shake to coat all of the chicken pieces. If freezing, skip to the storage instructions.

To cook, first let the chicken marinate for at least 3 hours in the refrigerator.

Preheat the oven to 350°F.

Line a baking sheet with aluminum foil. Place a wire rack on top of the foil.

Arrange the chicken pieces on the rack, reserving the marinade, and bake for 20 minutes. Turn the chicken pieces over, coating them on both sides with the reserved marinade, and bake for another 10 minutes. Turn the chicken once more, coat it on both sides with the reserved marinade, and bake for an additional 10 to 15 minutes, until the chicken is cooked through. Let rest for 5 minutes before serving.

TIP: If you don't have garam masala, substitute an Indian curry powder or curry paste. The flavor will be different but still delicious. You can also make your own custom garam masala by combining various spices in a grinder or mortar and pestle; look online for some basic recipes. It's simple, and there is nothing like a fresh spice blend.

TO REFRIGERATE: The uncooked chicken can be refrigerated in the marinade for up to 24 hours. To cook, follow the instructions above.

TO FREEZE: Freeze the raw chicken pieces in the marinade for up to three months. To serve, thaw in the refrigerator overnight, then cook per instructions above.

GLUTEN-FREE

SLOW COOKER MAPLE-MUSTARD CHICKEN

I like to serve this dish with brown rice, quinoa, or roasted sweet potatoes. The six-ingredient sweet-savory marinade tenderizes the chicken and infuses it with delectable flavor. For a simple vegetable side dish, sautéed green beans, roasted Brussels sprouts, or a green salad all complement the chicken equally well.

¼ cup pure maple syrup

¼ cup Dijon mustard

2 tablespoons balsamic vinegar

2 garlic cloves, minced

½ teaspoon kosher salt

½ teaspoon freshly ground black pepper

8 skinless, bone-in chicken drumsticks, thighs, or a combination

In a large, resealable plastic bag, mix together the maple syrup, mustard, vinegar, garlic, salt, and pepper. Add the chicken and toss to coat. Seal the bag, removing as much air as possible.

If freezing, skip ahead to the storage instructions. If not planning to freeze, refrigerate for about an hour to marinate.

To cook, transfer the chicken and marinade to a slow cooker, cover, and cook on high for about 4 hours or on low for 8 hours. Serve hot.

TIP: For a creamy sauce, remove the chicken legs from the slow cooker when they're finished cooking, then whisk 2 to 3 tablespoons of sour cream into the sauce. Leave the slow cooker uncovered and cook on high for about 15 minutes more, until the sauce thickens. Then return the chicken to the sauce to warm through.

TO REFRIGERATE: The raw chicken in the marinade can be refrigerated for up to 24 hours. Cook according to the instructions above.

TO FREEZE: Place the bag with the chicken and marinade in the freezer for up to three months. To cook, thaw in the refrigerator overnight or in a bowl of water for about an hour, changing the water once, then follow the cooking instructions above.

GLUTEN-FREE

DAIRY-FREE

110

SMOKED TURKEY AND PESTO PANINI WITH SUN-DRIED TOMATOES

SERVES 4 • PREP TIME: 5 MINUTES • COOK TIME: 10 MINUTES

This simple hot sandwich features smoked turkey, provolone cheese, tangy sun-dried tomatoes, and a smear of Fresh Basil Pesto (page 166, or substitute store-bought pesto).

8 slices whole-wheat sourdough bread

8 slices deli-sliced smoked turkey

8 ounces sliced cheese

12 sun-dried tomatoes packed in oil, drained, patted dry, and julienned

¼ cup Fresh Basil Pesto (page 166)

4 tablespoons olive oil or unsalted butter, divided

Arrange 4 bread slices on your work surface. Top each slice with 2 slices of turkey and 2 ounces of cheese. Divide the sun-dried tomatoes equally among the sandwiches. Spread about 1 tablespoon of pesto on each of the remaining 4 slices of bread and place them on top of the sandwiches. To store the sandwiches, skip ahead to the storage instructions.

To cook, heat 2 tablespoons of oil or butter in a large skillet over medium-high heat. Add the sandwiches to the skillet, and reduce the heat to medium. Cover and cook for 3 to 4 minutes, until the bottom is browned and the cheese is beginning to melt.

Add the remaining 2 tablespoons of oil or butter to the pan, and flip the sandwiches over. Cover the skillet, and cook for an additional 3 to 4 minutes, until the second side is browned and the cheese is melted. Cut each sandwich diagonally in half, and serve hot.

GLUTEN-FREE: Swap out the sourdough for gluten-free bread.

TIP: Use a panini maker, if you have one, to cook the sandwiches. Since they cook both sides at once, the total cooking time is cut in half.

TO REFRIGERATE: The uncooked, wrapped sandwiches can be stored in the refrigerator for up to three days. To cook, follow the instructions, left.

TO FREEZE: Place the uncooked, wrapped sandwiches in a large, resealable plastic bag, and note that you'll need butter or olive oil for cooking. Keep frozen for up to three months. To cook, follow the directions, left, but add a few minutes to the cooking time of each side so the frozen sandwich can defrost.

STIR-FRIED SPICY CHICKEN WITH GREEN BEANS

SERVES 4 • PREP TIME: 10 MINUTES • COOK TIME: 20 MINUTES

A quick, spicy stir-fry makes a nutritious weeknight meal, but the prep can sometimes make even a straightforward dish like this seem out of reach. This recipe can be prepped ahead and frozen raw. Once thawed, it takes less than 20 minutes to get it on the table. Serve it over steamed rice garnished with chopped peanuts, if you like.

2 tablespoons dry sherry or rice wine

3 tablespoons soy sauce

2 teaspoons sugar

2 garlic cloves, minced

1 (1-inch) piece of fresh ginger, peeled and minced

1 teaspoon crushed red pepper or chili paste

3 tablespoons cooking oil, divided

1½ pounds skinless, boneless chicken breast, cut into bite-size pieces

1½ pounds green beans, trimmed and cut into 2-inch lengths

2 tablespoons cornstarch whisked with 2 tablespoons water

In a medium bowl, stir together the sherry or rice wine, soy sauce, sugar, garlic, ginger, red pepper or chili paste, and 1 tablespoon of oil. Add the chicken and stir to coat. If freezing, skip ahead to the storage instructions.

To cook, let the chicken marinate in the sauce mixture for 15 minutes. Heat a second tablespoon of oil in a large skillet over medium-high heat. Add the chicken, reserving the marinade, and cook, stirring, until the chicken is browned on the outside but not cooked through, about 4 minutes. Transfer the chicken to a plate.

Add the remaining tablespoon of oil to the skillet and add the green beans. Cook, stirring frequently, until they begin to soften, about 6 minutes. Return the chicken to the skillet, and cook for about 5 more minutes, until the chicken is fully cooked.

Add the sauce mixture to the pan, reduce the heat to medium, and let simmer for 5 minutes. Add the cornstarch slurry and cook, stirring, for a few minutes more, until the sauce thickens. Serve hot.

GLUTEN-FREE: Substitute gluten-free tamari for the soy sauce.

TO REFRIGERATE: Cook the chicken as directed and let cool to room temperature. Store, covered, in the refrigerator for up to three days. To serve, reheat in the microwave or in a skillet on the stovetop over medium heat.

TO FREEZE: Transfer the chicken-and-marinade mixture to a large, resealable plastic bag, then prepare the green beans and put them in a separate plastic bag. Store both bags together in one extra-large, resealable plastic bag. Make a note on the label that you'll need two tablespoons each of cooking oil and cornstarch to complete the dish. To serve, thaw the bag in the refrigerator overnight or in a bowl of water for up to an hour, changing the water once. Cook according to instructions at left.

DAIRY-FREE

THAI-STYLE RED CURRY CHICKEN

Think of curry paste as a "secret" ingredient for creating flavorful dishes without a lot of fuss. Thai curry paste contains chiles, lemongrass, kaffir lime leaves, and other seasonings that lend your dish multiple layers of complex flavor, all with just a few spoonfuls of one ingredient. Be careful, though—the spiciness of curry paste can vary widely among brands, so start with a little and add more to taste.

1 (15-ounce) can coconut milk, stirred

2 to 4 tablespoons Thai red curry paste

2 tablespoons brown sugar

1 tablespoon fish sauce

3 tablespoons coconut or other cooking
    oil, divided

1½ pounds boneless, skinless chicken breasts, cut
    into bite-size pieces

1½ pounds mixed vegetables (any combination
    will work including broccoli florets, sliced
    carrots, diced bell peppers, bamboo shoots,
    or any other vegetables you like in stir-fries)

In a medium bowl, combine the coconut milk, curry paste, brown sugar, and fish sauce, and stir to mix. If planning to freeze, skip ahead to the storage instructions.

To cook, heat 1 tablespoon of oil in a large skillet and cook the chicken, stirring frequently, for about 4 minutes, until it's lightly browned on the outside but not cooked through. Transfer the chicken to a plate.

Heat the remaining 2 tablespoons of oil in the skillet and add the vegetables. Cook, stirring frequently, until they begin to soften, about 6 minutes. Add the sauce mixture and bring to a boil. Reduce the heat to medium-low and let simmer until the sauce thickens and the vegetables are tender, about 5 minutes more. Add the chicken back to the skillet, and cook, stirring occasionally, until the chicken is cooked through, about another 5 minutes. Serve hot.

PALEO: Use honey instead of brown sugar.

TIP: A bag of frozen stir-fry vegetables works just as well as fresh vegetables.

TO REFRIGERATE: Let the dish cool to room temperature, then store, covered, in the refrigerator for up to three days. To serve, reheat in a skillet on the stovetop over medium heat, or in the microwave.

TO FREEZE: Place the sauce mixture, the chicken, and the vegetables in separate resealable plastic bags, remove as much air as possible, and seal. Store all three elements of the dish together in one extra-large, resealable plastic bag for up to three months. To serve, thaw in the refrigerator overnight or in a bowl of water for up to an hour, changing the water once. Follow the cooking instructions at left.

GLUTEN-FREE

DAIRY-FREE

CHICKEN-AND-SPINACH ENCHILADAS IN RED CHILE SAUCE

SERVES 4 • PREP TIME: 10 MINUTES • COOK TIME: 20 MINUTES

This enchilada recipe is quick to whip together, especially if you have leftover cooked chicken and Red Chile Sauce (page 161). Serve with traditional toppings like a dollop of guacamole or sour cream, with hot sauce on the side for some extra kick.

2 cups Red Chile Sauce (page 161)

1 pound shredded cooked chicken

1 (10-ounce) package frozen spinach, thawed, drained, and squeezed to release excess moisture

10 corn tortillas

2 ½ cups (about 12 ounces) shredded cheese (Monterey Jack, Cheddar, or a Mexican cheese blend)

Cover the bottom of two 8-by-8-inch baking dishes or one 9-by-13-inch baking dish with several spoonfuls of Red Chile Sauce.

In a medium bowl, stir together the chicken, spinach, and about ½ cup of Red Chile Sauce.

Wrap the tortillas in a damp dishtowel and heat in the microwave for about 30 seconds to soften them.

Fill each tortilla with about ½ cup of the chicken mixture and roll up. Place the filled tortillas in the baking dish, seam-side down. Once all the tortillas are filled, rolled, and placed in the baking dish, pour the remaining sauce over the top. If freezing the enchiladas before cooking, skip ahead to the storage instructions.

To cook, preheat the oven to 375°F.

Sprinkle the cheese evenly over the top of the enchiladas and bake for about 20 minutes, until the cheese is melted and bubbly. Serve hot, or cool to room temperature before storing.

DAIRY-FREE: Omit the cheese or use soy cheese.

TIP: If you're planning to freeze the enchiladas, line the baking dish with parchment paper or aluminum foil before assembling. This will make it easy to lift the enchiladas from the baking dish once they're frozen, for easy storage.

TO REFRIGERATE: The baked enchiladas can be refrigerated, covered, for up to three days. To reheat, either heat in the microwave, or cover the baking dish with aluminum foil and bake in a 375°F oven for about 15 minutes, until heated through.

TO FREEZE: For uncooked enchiladas, cover the baking dish tightly with aluminum foil or plastic wrap, and freeze until solid. Once frozen, remove the enchiladas from the dish, wrap them tightly in foil or plastic wrap, and store in the freezer for up to three months. Store the shredded cheese along with the enchiladas in a resealable plastic bag. To cook from frozen, remove the plastic wrap, place in a baking dish, and sprinkle the cheese over the top. Then cover the dish with aluminum foil and bake in a 375°F oven for about 50 minutes, until heated through. To brown the top, remove the foil about 15 minutes before the end of cooking or put under the broiler for a few minutes. Serve hot.

Cooked enchiladas can also be frozen—covered in the baking dish, wrapped in foil or plastic wrap, or wrapped in individual portions—for up to three months. Reheat frozen cooked enchiladas covered with foil in a 375°F oven for about 35 minutes, until heated through, or reheat them in the microwave.

CHICKEN BREAST IN CHIMICHURRI SAUCE

SERVES 4 • PREP TIME: 15 MINUTES, PLUS 2 HOURS TO MARINATE • COOK TIME: 10 MINUTES

Chimichurri is an Argentinian sauce made from fresh herbs, garlic, vinegar, and olive oil, usually served on grilled meats. Any leftovers of this tender, juicy chicken dish are perfect for adding to a salad or sandwich.

4 boneless, skinless chicken breasts

2 cups (packed) flat-leaf parsley leaves

¼ cup (packed) fresh oregano leaves

4 garlic cloves, smashed

¼ cup red-wine vinegar

½ teaspoon crushed red pepper

½ teaspoon kosher salt

1 cup olive oil

Put the chicken breasts between two sheets of parchment paper and pound them to an even thickness.

In a food processor, combine the parsley, oregano, garlic, vinegar, red pepper, and salt, and pulse until finely chopped. With the food processor running, add the oil in a slow, steady stream, stopping to scrape down the sides of the bowl as needed. Process until well combined. If freezing, skip to the storage instructions below.

To serve, in a medium bowl, combine the chicken with half of the sauce mixture and refrigerate, covered, for at least 2 hours.

Heat a grill or grill pan to high heat. Remove the chicken from the marinade, and grill for 2 to 3 minutes per side, until grill marks appear and the chicken is cooked through. Serve immediately, topped with the remaining chimichurri sauce.

TO REFRIGERATE: The uncooked chicken in marinade can be stored, covered, in the refrigerator for up to 24 hours, while the sauce on its own can be stored in the refrigerator for up to three days. To serve, follow the instructions, left. When cooked, the chicken can be stored in the refrigerator for up to three days. Serve cold or at room temperature in a sandwich or salad with the sauce drizzled over the top.

TO FREEZE: Place the uncooked chicken and half of the sauce mixture in a large, resealable plastic bag. Seal the bag, removing as much air as possible. Then transfer the remaining sauce mixture to another small, resealable plastic bag. Seal tightly and freeze flat. Store the chicken and sauce together in the freezer for up to three months. To serve, thaw in the refrigerator overnight or in a bowl of water for up to an hour, changing the water once. Follow the cooking instructions, left.

PALEO

GLUTEN-FREE

DAIRY-FREE

HOISIN CHICKEN IN LETTUCE CUPS

SERVES 4 • PREP TIME: 10 MINUTES • COOK TIME: 10 MINUTES

This flavorful chicken recipe takes only 20 minutes from start to finish, but you can also freeze it before cooking. I love the contrast between the hot, juicy chicken and the crisp lettuce leaves, but you can also serve the chicken over cooked brown rice.

¼ cup plus 2 tablespoons hoisin sauce, divided

2 tablespoons water

1 tablespoon soy sauce

1 tablespoon dry sherry or white wine

2 tablespoons cooking oil

1 garlic clove, minced

2 teaspoons minced, peeled ginger

1 large carrot, finely diced

1 red bell pepper, finely diced

1½ pounds ground chicken

8 large lettuce leaves, such as iceberg, butter, or romaine

In a small bowl, combine 2 tablespoons hoisin sauce with the water, soy sauce, and sherry.

Heat the oil in a large skillet over medium-high heat. Add the garlic and ginger and cook, stirring, for 1 minute. Add the carrot and bell pepper and cook, stirring frequently, for about 5 minutes. Add the ground chicken and cook, stirring, until it's opaque. Add the sauce mixture and cook, stirring, for about 3 minutes, until the sauce thickens and heats through.

Serve hot, spooning the mixture into the lettuce leaves and drizzling the remaining ¼ cup hoisin sauce over the top as desired.

TIP: If you find the sauce too thin, mix 2 teaspoons of cornstarch with 2 teaspoons of water until there are no lumps, and whisk it into the pan during the last few minutes of cooking. The sauce should thicken up quickly.

TO REFRIGERATE: The cooked chicken can be stored in the refrigerator for up to three days. To serve, reheat in a large skillet over medium heat.

TO FREEZE: To freeze before cooking, store the ground chicken in a resealable plastic bag, the sauce mixture in a second plastic bag, and the chopped carrots, bell pepper, ginger, and garlic in a third. Store all three bags in one large, resealable plastic bag, and note on the bag that you'll need fresh lettuce leaves and hoisin sauce for serving. The uncooked components can be stored in the freezer for up to three months. To serve, thaw in the refrigerator overnight or in a bowl of cold water for up to an hour, changing the water once.

To freeze the dish after cooking, follow the recipe, then let the chicken cool to room temperature. Store in a large, resealable plastic bag, and freeze flat for up to three months. Make a note on the package that you'll need fresh lettuce leaves and hoisin sauce for serving. To serve, thaw in the refrigerator overnight or in a bowl of cold water for up to an hour, changing the water once. Reheat in a large skillet over medium heat.

DAIRY-FREE

117

POULTRY

MEXICAN-STYLE MEATBALLS (PAGE 128)

chapter eight

MEAT

HONEY-ORANGE ROAST PORK LOIN

Season a pork roast, mix up a quick marinade, combine the two, and stash them in the freezer to cook later. You can choose between using a slow cooker and roasting in the oven; either way, the cooking is almost completely hands-off. Serve this pork roast with a side of quinoa and sautéed or steamed green beans.

1 (2-pound) boneless pork loin roast

1 teaspoon kosher salt

½ teaspoon freshly ground pepper

¼ cup honey

Zest and juice of 1 orange

2 tablespoons olive oil

1½ teaspoons minced fresh thyme or ½ teaspoon dried thyme

½ cup chicken broth

Season the pork roast all over with the salt and pepper.

In a small bowl, whisk together the honey, orange zest and juice, olive oil, thyme, and chicken broth. To refrigerate or freeze before cooking, skip ahead to the storage instructions.

To cook in a slow cooker, place the pork roast in the slow cooker and pour the sauce mixture over the top. Cook on low for 8 hours or on high for 4 hours.

To roast in the oven, preheat the oven to 375°F. Place the pork roast in a roasting pan or Dutch oven and pour the marinade over the top. Roast in the preheated oven for 1½ to 2 hours, until cooked through. Let rest for 10 minutes before slicing and serving.

GLUTEN-FREE: Use gluten-free broth.

TO REFRIGERATE: In either a large bowl or a large, resealable plastic bag, pour the marinade over the pork roast. Cover or seal and store in the refrigerator for up to two days. To cook, follow the cooking instructions at left.

TO FREEZE: Place the uncooked pork roast in a large, resealable plastic bag. Pour the marinade over the top and make sure the pork is fully coated. Seal the bag, removing as much air as possible. Store in the freezer for up to three months. To serve, thaw overnight in the refrigerator, then follow the cooking instructions at left.

PALEO

DAIRY-FREE

APPLE-STUFFED PORK LOIN WITH BACON

SERVES 6 TO 8 • PREP TIME: 10 MINUTES • COOK TIME: 1½ HOURS (OVEN)
OR 8 HOURS (SLOW COOKER)

This pork roast is bursting with all kinds of tempting flavors—sweet apples, smoky bacon, brown sugar, and spicy mustard. Round out the meal with sautéed greens and a side of roasted or mashed sweet potatoes.

1 (3-pound) pork loin roast
Kosher salt
Freshly ground black pepper
2 large apples, sliced
¼ cup light brown sugar
¼ cup apple juice
1 tablespoon Dijon mustard
6 strips bacon

Cut the pork loin into 1-inch slices, cutting only about three-quarters of the way through so that the whole roast is still connected at the bottom. Season the roast all over with salt and pepper.

Stuff the apple slices into the pockets you've made in the roast. In a small bowl, stir together the brown sugar, apple juice, and mustard, and pour the mixture over the top of the roast.

Lay the bacon pieces on top. To freeze or refrigerate uncooked, skip ahead to the storage instructions.

To cook in a slow cooker, place the roast in the slow cooker, cover, and cook on low for 8 hours or on high for 4 hours.

To cook in the oven, preheat the oven to 375°F. Place the roast in a roasting pan or Dutch oven, and cook, uncovered, for about 1½ hours, until the roast is cooked through.

TO REFRIGERATE: Wrap the uncooked roast tightly in plastic wrap or place it in a resealable plastic bag. Refrigerate for up to two days. To cook, follow the instructions above.

TO FREEZE: Place the uncooked roast in a resealable plastic bag and freeze for up to three months. To cook, thaw in the refrigerator for at least 24 hours, until fully thawed, and then follow the instructions above.

GLUTEN-FREE

DAIRY-FREE

SEARED PORK CHOPS WITH CRANBERRIES AND THYME

SERVES 4 • PREP TIME: 10 MINUTES • COOK TIME: 50 MINUTES

These pork chops are loaded with flavor, and the cranberries give them just a touch of sweetness and acidity. Serve them with rice pilaf and roasted Brussels sprouts to complete a hearty meal.

4 boneless pork chops, about ½ inch thick

½ teaspoon kosher salt

¼ teaspoon freshly ground black pepper

2 tablespoons unsalted butter

½ cup chopped onion

1 garlic clove, minced

½ cup chicken broth or water

1 cup fresh or frozen cranberries

3 sprigs fresh thyme

2 tablespoons (packed) brown sugar

Season the pork chops on both sides with salt and pepper.

Melt the butter in a large skillet set over medium heat. Add the pork chops and cook for about 5 minutes per side, until nicely browned and cooked through. Transfer the chops from the pan to a plate.

Add the onion and garlic to the skillet, and cook, stirring, until soft, about 5 minutes. Add the broth or water to the skillet and bring to a boil, stirring and scraping up any browned bits stuck to the bottom of the skillet. Stir in the cranberries, thyme, and brown sugar, and simmer over medium-low heat until the cranberries break down, about 40 minutes. To store, skip ahead to the storage instructions.

To serve, return the pork chops, along with any accumulated juices, to the skillet and cook until heated through. Serve hot.

GLUTEN-FREE: Use gluten-free broth or water.

TO REFRIGERATE: Let the sauce cool to room temperature, then combine it with the pork chops. Store, covered, in the refrigerator for up to three days. To serve, reheat in a skillet on the stovetop or in the microwave.

TO FREEZE: Let the sauce cool to room temperature, then combine it in a large, resealable plastic bag with the pork chops. Seal the bag, removing as much air as possible, and freeze for up to three months. To serve, thaw in the refrigerator overnight. Reheat in a skillet on the stovetop or in the microwave.

SLOW COOKER PULLED PORK

Slow-cooking pork keeps it from drying out, resulting in tender, juicy meat perfect for multiple uses, like shredding over tortilla chips for meaty nachos, or drenching with barbecue sauce and stuffing into a sandwich roll alongside Tangy Coleslaw (page 152).

1 tablespoon (packed) dark brown sugar

1 tablespoon chili powder

1 tablespoon kosher salt

½ teaspoon ground cumin

¼ teaspoon cinnamon

1 (4 ½-to-5-pound) boneless pork shoulder

2 onions, thinly sliced

4 garlic cloves, thinly sliced

1 cup chicken broth

In a small bowl, combine the sugar, chili powder, salt, cumin, and cinnamon. Pat the pork shoulder dry and then rub the spice mixture all over it. To freeze or refrigerate for later, skip ahead to the storage instructions below.

To cook, place the onions, garlic, and broth in the slow cooker. Place the spice-rubbed pork on top. Cover and cook on low for 8 to 10 hours or on high for 6 to 8 hours, until the meat is very tender and falls apart easily when you test it with a fork.

Transfer the pork to a cutting board or a large bowl, and use two forks to shred the meat.

Empty the onions from the slow cooker into a colander set over a bowl to strain out the liquid. (Reserve the liquid.) Return the onions to the slow cooker along with the shredded meat. Add the strained liquid back to the pot, a few spoonfuls at a time, and mix until the meat is moistened. Discard any remaining liquid. Serve hot.

GLUTEN-FREE: Use gluten-free broth.

TO REFRIGERATE: Place the onions, garlic, broth, and spice-rubbed pork into a large, resealable plastic bag. Refrigerate for up to 24 hours. Cook and serve per instructions, left.

TO FREEZE: Place the onions, garlic, broth, and spice-rubbed pork into a large, resealable plastic bag and freeze for up to three months. To cook and serve, thaw the pork in the refrigerator for at least 24 hours, until completely thawed. Follow cooking instructions, left.

DAIRY-FREE

SLOW COOKER PULLED PORK TACO KITS

SERVES 4 • PREP TIME: 10 MINUTES • COOK TIME: 10 MINUTES

Tacos are a terrific, speedy meal, especially when all the elements are pre-prepared and ready to go. This recipe combines the Slow Cooker Pulled Pork (page 123) with Red Chile Sauce (page 161), but you could use a jarred enchilada sauce instead. Serve Mexican rice and refried beans alongside for a filling meal.

FOR THE TACO KITS
1¼ pounds shredded Slow Cooker Pulled Pork (page 123)
¾ cup Red Chile Sauce (page 161)

FOR SERVING
12 soft corn tortillas
2 cups shredded cheese (Monterey Jack, pepper Jack, Cheddar, or a mixture)
¼ head green cabbage, very thinly sliced
1 cup salsa
½ cup chopped cilantro
1 lime, cut into wedges

In a large bowl, stir the pork and Red Chile Sauce until well mixed. To store, skip ahead to the storage instructions.

Preheat the oven to 400°F.

Wrap the tortillas in aluminum foil and heat in the oven for about 10 minutes.

Meanwhile, heat the pork-and-sauce mixture in a large skillet or saucepan over medium heat.

Fill the tortillas with the pork mixture, and top with some of the cheese and cabbage. Garnish with salsa, cilantro, and a lime wedge, and serve immediately.

TO REFRIGERATE: Store the pork and sauce mixture, covered, in the refrigerator for up to three days, along with the cheese, cabbage, tortillas, and garnishes. To serve, follow the instructions above.

TO FREEZE: Transfer the pork mixture to a large, resealable plastic bag. Remove as much air as possible and seal. Put the shredded cheese, cabbage, and tortillas in separate, resealable plastic bags. Store all four bags together in one large, resealable plastic bag in the freezer for up to three months. To serve, thaw the pork in the refrigerator overnight or in the microwave. Follow the heating and serving instructions above.

GLUTEN-FREE

THE HEALTHY MAKE-AHEAD COOKBOOK

PORK WITH PEANUT SAUCE

Peanut butter, stirred into the sauce after cooking, gives this slightly spicy pork a rich, nutty flavor. Serve it over steamed brown rice or toss with noodles.

¼ cup creamy peanut butter

3 tablespoons soy sauce

3 tablespoons brown sugar

2 tablespoons rice vinegar

2 garlic cloves, minced

1 teaspoon crushed red pepper

2 tablespoons cooking oil

2 pounds pork tenderloin, cut into bite-size pieces

In a small bowl, combine the peanut butter, soy sauce, brown sugar, vinegar, garlic, and crushed red pepper.

To freeze or refrigerate before cooking, skip ahead to the storage instructions.

To cook, heat the oil in a large skillet over medium-high heat. Add the pork and cook, stirring, until browned on all sides, about 5 minutes. Add the sauce mixture to the pan, and bring to a boil. Cook until the sauce thickens and the pork is cooked through, about 8 minutes. Serve hot.

TO REFRIGERATE: Pour the sauce mixture in a small covered container. Put the pork in a second covered container. Make a note that you'll need cooking oil to finish the dish. Refrigerate for up to 24 hours. To cook, follow the instructions, left.

TO FREEZE: Pour the sauce mixture into a pint-size resealable plastic bag. Put the pork in a quart-size resealable plastic bag. Store the two bags in one gallon-size resealable plastic bag. Make a note that you'll need cooking oil to finish the dish. Freeze for up to three months. To cook, thaw the bags in the refrigerator overnight or in a bowl of water for up to an hour, changing the water once. Follow the cooking instructions, left.

DAIRY-FREE

CLASSIC MEAT LOAF

SERVES 4 • PREP TIME: 10 MINUTES • COOK TIME: 1 HOUR

This meat loaf certainly isn't fancy, but it is the perfect comfort food, especially if you serve it with mashed potatoes and gravy. Plus you can add bacon, hot sauce, salsa, chili powder, Italian seasoning, diced bell peppers—virtually any flavors you love. It's also easily doubled, and leftovers make great sandwiches.

1½ pounds lean ground beef

¾ cup instant oatmeal

¾ cup milk

1 small onion, finely diced

1 tablespoon Worcestershire sauce

1 teaspoon kosher salt

½ teaspoon freshly ground pepper

1 large egg

⅓ cup ketchup

In a large bowl, mix together all the ingredients. Transfer the ingredients to a 9-by-5-inch loaf pan. (Line the pan with plastic wrap or aluminum foil before adding the meat mixture if you plan to freeze the meat loaf before baking; this will make it easy to lift it out of the pan for storage.) If you're planning to refrigerate the uncooked meat loaf, skip ahead to the storage instructions below.

To cook, preheat the oven to 350°F. Bake the meat loaf, uncovered, in the preheated oven for about 1 hour, until cooked through. Let it stand for 10 to 15 minutes before slicing and serving.

TIP: You can also opt to make several smaller loaves instead of one large one. See Cajun-Spiced Turkey Mini Meat Loaves (page 104) for cooking times.

TO REFRIGERATE: The uncooked meat loaf can be stored, covered, in the refrigerator for up to 24 hours. To cook, follow the instructions above.

TO FREEZE: Wrap the meat loaf tightly with plastic wrap or aluminum foil and freeze for up to three months. To cook, place the frozen meat loaf back into the loaf pan in which it was formed, or place it on a baking sheet. Bake, uncovered, in a 350°F oven for about 1½ hours, until cooked through. You can also thaw the meat loaf first in the refrigerator for at least 24 hours, then cook following the instructions above.

INSIDE-OUT CHEESEBURGERS

SERVES 8 • PREP TIME: 15 MINUTES • COOK TIME: 10 MINUTES

You can certainly buy frozen, preformed burger patties, but since they're unseasoned, they lack flavor. These patties, on the other hand, are made with a flavorful seasoned beef mixture and stuffed with cheese that melts into a gooey delicious center as the burgers cook. Serve them on lightly toasted buns along with your favorite burger toppings. Add a side of oven-baked Spicy Sweet Potato Fries (page 150) to round out the meal.

3 pounds ground chuck

1 onion, finely diced

2 teaspoons kosher salt

2 teaspoons freshly ground black pepper

¼ cup Worcestershire sauce

8 ounces shredded cheese (any type, such as Cheddar, Swiss, or Gruyère)

To make the patties, in a large bowl, combine the beef, onion, salt, pepper, and Worcestershire sauce. Form the mixture into 16 equally sized patties, about ¼ inch thick. Lay 8 of the patties on your work surface, and divide the shredded cheese among them, piling the cheese in the center of the patties. Place the remaining 8 patties on top of the cheese-topped patties, and press to join them so that the cheese is in the middle. To refrigerate or freeze before cooking, skip ahead to the storage instructions.

To cook, heat a grill, grill pan, or large skillet to medium-high heat, and cook the burgers for about 4 minutes on each side. Serve hot on lightly toasted buns, topped with your favorite burger toppings.

TO REFRIGERATE: Cover the patties tightly with plastic wrap and refrigerate for up to 24 hours. To cook, follow the directions above.

TO FREEZE: Place the patties on a large, parchment paper-lined baking sheet, cover tightly with plastic wrap, and freeze until solid, at least two hours. Transfer the frozen patties to a large, resealable plastic bag, placing squares of parchment paper between them to prevent sticking. Seal the bag tightly, removing as much air as possible, and freeze for up to three months. (Note on the bag that you'll need burger buns and condiments for serving, if necessary.) To cook, thaw the burgers completely in the refrigerator overnight and follow the instructions above, or cook directly from frozen, adding additional cooking time. Frozen burgers will take 8 to 10 minutes per side to cook through.

MEXICAN-STYLE MEATBALLS

SERVES 8 (ABOUT 40 MEATBALLS) • PREP TIME: 20 MINUTES • COOK TIME: 30 MINUTES

These Mexican-Style Meatballs are every bit as delicious as the Italian-style meatballs everyone loves, but feature south-of-the-border seasonings. Serve over rice, topped with Red Chile Sauce (page 161) and additional cotija or feta cheese, or in a Mexican-style soup.

1 white onion, coarsely chopped

2 garlic cloves

1 (3½-ounce) can diced fire-roasted green chiles, drained

½ cup (packed) cilantro

2 corn tortillas, torn into pieces

2 large eggs

1 cup (about 4 ounces) crumbled cotija or feta cheese

2 teaspoons kosher salt

1 teaspoon ground cumin

2 pounds ground chuck

In a food processor, pulse the onion and garlic until coarsely chopped. Add the green chiles, cilantro, and tortillas, and pulse until finely chopped.

In a large bowl, combine the eggs, cheese, salt, cumin, and meat. Add the onion-and-green-chile mixture, and mix until well combined.

Form the mixture into 1½-inch balls, and arrange them in a single layer on a large baking sheet. If freezing or refrigerating, skip ahead to the storage instructions.

To cook, preheat the oven to 400°F. Bake the meatballs, uncovered, for 25 to 30 minutes, until browned on the outside and cooked through. Serve hot, or cool to room temperature to store.

GLUTEN-FREE

TIP: For different flavors, vary the type of meat. I find that ground turkey or chicken makes delicious but lighter meatballs. For added flavor, substitute ground pork or loose Italian sausage for half of the beef.

TO REFRIGERATE: Store uncooked meatballs, covered, in the refrigerator for up to 24 hours. To cook, follow the directions above.

Cooked meatballs can be refrigerated, covered, for up to three days. Reheat in the microwave or in a covered baking dish in a 400°F oven, or simmer in a sauce, such as Red Chile Sauce (page 161), in a saucepan on the stovetop.

TO FREEZE: Freeze uncooked meatballs on the baking sheet for at least two hours, until frozen solid. Transfer to a large, resealable plastic bag, and keep in the freezer for up to three months. These frozen uncooked meatballs can be cooked in soup or sauce by simmering them for about 25 minutes. They can also be cooked in a 400°F oven on a baking sheet for about 45 minutes, until cooked through and browned on the outside.

For cooked meatballs, freeze on a baking sheet, then transfer to a large, resealable plastic bag and store in the freezer for up to three months. Reheat in a sauce or in a covered dish in the microwave.

STEAK FAJITAS

SERVES 8 • PREP TIME: 10 MINUTES, PLUS AT LEAST 30 MINUTES
TO MARINATE • COOK TIME: 10 MINUTES

Flank-steak fajitas make a festive meal. You can prep everything ahead of time and cook this dish straight from the freezer. Just add your favorite toppings—guacamole, salsa, sour cream—and you're all set.

¼ cup freshly squeezed lime juice

2 teaspoons chili powder

1½ teaspoons kosher salt

2 pounds skirt or flank steak, thinly sliced against the grain

1 onion, thinly sliced

2 bell peppers (red, green, orange, or a combination), seeded and thinly sliced

2 jalapeños, seeded and thinly sliced into rings (optional)

2 tablespoons cooking oil

8 flour tortillas, for serving

In a large bowl, combine the lime juice, chili powder, and salt. Add the meat, onion, bell peppers, and jalapeños (if using), and toss to coat. To freeze, skip ahead to the storage instructions below.

To cook, let the mixture marinate in the refrigerator for at least 30 minutes.

Heat the oil in a large skillet over medium-high heat. Add the meat and vegetables, discarding the marinating liquid. Cook, stirring occasionally, for about 8 minutes, until the meat is browned and cooked through, and the vegetables are soft. Serve hot, with warm tortillas.

GLUTEN-FREE: Use corn tortillas or omit the tortillas entirely.

TO REFRIGERATE: Store the meat and vegetable mixture, covered, in the refrigerator for up to 24 hours. To cook, follow the instructions above.

TO FREEZE: Transfer the meat, vegetables, and marinade to one or two large, resealable plastic bags, removing as much air as possible. Freeze flat and store in the freezer for up to three months. The tortillas can also be frozen in a separate resealable plastic bag.

To cook, heat the oil in a skillet over medium-high heat. Add the frozen meat and vegetables from the bag, and cook, covered, for about 10 minutes. Remove the cover and continue to cook about 5 minutes more, until the meat is browned and cooked through, the vegetables are soft, and the liquid has evaporated.

DAIRY-FREE

LAMB OR BEEF-STUFFED EGGPLANT IN TOMATO SAUCE

SERVES 4 • PREP TIME: 15 MINUTES • COOK TIME: 55 MINUTES

Both eggplant and ground meat stand up especially well to freezing. The Greek-inspired seasoning in this dish equally complements both beef and lamb, so use whichever you prefer. For a lower-fat dish, you could even substitute ground turkey. Garnish with some chopped mint leaves for an especially fresh touch.

Cooking oil, to prepare the baking dish
2 large eggplants, halved lengthwise
1 tablespoon unsalted butter
1 pound ground lamb or beef
½ onion, diced
2 garlic cloves, minced
1 (14 ½-ounce) can diced tomatoes
1 tablespoon tomato paste
½ teaspoon cinnamon
½ teaspoon kosher salt
½ teaspoon freshly ground pepper
2 cups Marinara Sauce (page 163) or jarred
    tomato sauce

Preheat the oven to 350°F.

Lightly oil a 9-by-13-inch baking dish.

Scoop out the eggplant flesh, leaving about a ¼-inch layer of flesh inside the skin. Chop the scooped-out flesh and set aside.

In a large skillet, melt the butter over medium-high heat. Add the eggplant skins, cut-side down, and cook for about 5 minutes. Turn the skins over and cook the other side for 5 minutes more. Arrange the skins cut-side up in the prepared baking dish.

Add the meat to the skillet and cook, stirring, for about 5 minutes, until browned. Remove the meat from the pan, draining off the excess fat. Add the onion and garlic to the skillet, and cook, stirring frequently, until soft, about 5 minutes. Add the chopped eggplant flesh and cook, stirring occasionally, for 5 minutes more. Return the meat to the pan along with the tomatoes, tomato paste, cinnamon, salt, and pepper. Stir to mix well and let simmer over medium heat for an additional 5 minutes.

Spoon the meat mixture into the eggplant skins in the baking dish. Then spoon the sauce over the top, dividing equally, and bake in the preheated oven for 30 minutes. Cut each eggplant half in two and serve hot. If freezing or refrigerating, let cool to room temperature before storing.

TIP: This dish is even more delicious with feta cheese sprinkled over the sauced eggplant halves before baking.

TO REFRIGERATE: Cover the cooked, stuffed eggplants and refrigerate for up to three days. To serve, follow the instructions above.

TO FREEZE: Halve the stuffed eggplants, and place each half in an individual freezer container (or freeze them all in one large container). Freeze for up to three months. To serve, thaw in the refrigerator overnight or in the microwave, then reheat, covered, in a 350°F oven for about 30 minutes, until heated through.

GLUTEN-FREE

THAI-STYLE BEEF CURRY WITH COCONUT MILK

SERVES 8 • PREP TIME: 10 MINUTES • COOK TIME: 20 MINUTES

In this perfect balance of hot and creamy flavors, spicy Thai red curry paste is mellowed by rich coconut milk and peanut butter. You can assemble and freeze the entire dish raw, so all you need to do is thaw it and then stir-fry it in a skillet. Serve this curry over cooked brown rice, and garnish with fresh basil or cilantro.

1 cup coconut milk

¼ cup peanut butter

3 tablespoons brown sugar

2 tablespoons fresh lime juice

1 to 2 tablespoons Thai red curry paste

1 tablespoon fish sauce

½ teaspoon kosher salt

2 tablespoons cooking oil

2 pounds flank or skirt steak, cut into bite-size strips

½ pound green beans, cut into 1½-inch pieces

In a large bowl, combine the coconut milk, peanut butter, brown sugar, lime juice, curry paste, fish sauce, and salt, and stir to mix.

If you're freezing or refrigerating before cooking, skip ahead to the storage instructions.

To cook, heat the oil in a large skillet over medium-high heat. Add the beef and cook, stirring, until browned, about 5 minutes. Transfer the meat to a plate. Add the sauce mixture and the green beans to the pan, and bring to a boil. Cook, stirring, for about 10 minutes, until the sauce thickens and the green beans are tender. Return the meat to the pan, along with any accumulated juices, and cook, stirring, for about 3 minutes more, until the meat is heated through. Serve hot.

TO REFRIGERATE: Place the sauce mixture in a small covered container and the beef in a second covered container. Store the green beans in a plastic bag, and make a note that you'll need cooking oil to finish the dish. Refrigerate all the components for up to 24 hours. To cook, follow the instructions, left.

TO FREEZE: Place the sauce mixture in a pint-size resealable plastic bag and the beef in a quart-size resealable plastic bag. Put the green beans in a separate quart-size resealable plastic bag. Store all three bags in one gallon-size resealable plastic bag, and make a note that you'll need cooking oil to finish the dish. Freeze for up to three months. To cook, thaw the bags overnight in the refrigerator or in a bowl of water for up to an hour, changing the water once. Follow the cooking instructions, left.

GLUTEN-FREE

THE HEALTHY MAKE-AHEAD COOKBOOK

SHEPHERD'S PIE WITH SWEET POTATO TOPPING

SERVES 4 • PREP TIME: 15 MINUTES • COOK TIME: 45 MINUTES

Shepherd's pie is a rustic English dish made of ground meat (traditionally lamb, but this recipe calls for beef), cooked with vegetables and topped with a layer of mashed potatoes. I've substituted mashed sweet potatoes to make the dish a bit more nutritious—but just as delicious. This dish freezes well either in one large portion or in smaller, individual portions. It is also easily doubled.

1 pound lean ground beef

1 large onion, diced

2 large carrots, peeled and diced

¾ teaspoon freshly ground black pepper

1½ teaspoons kosher salt, divided

1 cup fresh or frozen peas

5 tablespoons unsalted butter, divided

2 tablespoons all-purpose flour

1 cup beef broth

2 pounds sweet potatoes, peeled and cut into large cubes

¾ cup half-and-half

Heat a large skillet over medium-high heat. Add the beef and cook, stirring frequently, until the beef is browned, about 5 minutes. Drain excess fat.

Stir in the onion, carrot, pepper, and ¾ teaspoon of salt, and cook, stirring occasionally, until the vegetables are tender, about 10 minutes. Stir in the peas, and cook for 2 more minutes. Add 2 tablespoons of butter, and cook, stirring, until melted. Sprinkle in the flour, and cook, stirring, for 1 more minute.

Add the broth, bring to a boil, and simmer for about 2 minutes, until the sauce thickens. Transfer the meat mixture to an 8-by-8-inch baking dish. (If planning to freeze, line the baking dish with plastic wrap first.)

To make the topping, cook the sweet potato cubes in boiling water for about 5 minutes, until tender. Drain well. In a large bowl, mash the sweet potatoes with the remaining 3 tablespoons of butter, the half-and-half, and the remaining ¾ teaspoon of salt. Spread the mashed sweet potatoes in an even layer over the meat mixture in the baking dish. If freezing or refrigerating, let cool to room temperature, and skip ahead to the storage instructions. »

To cook, preheat the oven to 425°F.

Bake the shepherd's pie for about 25 minutes, until the topping is golden brown and crisp. Serve hot.

TIP: If you're short on time for prep, pop the whole, unpeeled sweet potatoes in the microwave and cook for 5 to 10 minutes, until soft (do this while preparing the meat mixture). The peels will slip right off, and you'll be ready to make your mash.

TO REFRIGERATE: Cover the dish tightly and refrigerate for up to three days. To serve, follow the cooking instructions at left.

TO FREEZE: Cover the baking dish tightly with foil or plastic wrap and freeze for up to three months. (For easier storage, line the pan with plastic wrap to lift the shepherd's pie out of the baking dish once it's frozen.) To serve, reheat the frozen shepherd's pie in the baking dish, covered with aluminum foil, in a 350°F oven for about one hour. Alternatively, thaw the pie in the refrigerator for 24 hours, then reheat in the baking dish, covered with aluminum foil, in a 350°F oven for about 30 minutes.

SLOW COOKER SPICED BEEF WITH DRIED APRICOTS

SERVES 6 • PREP TIME: 10 MINUTES • COOK TIME: 8 HOURS

Slowly cooked all day, this hearty beef stew becomes loaded with complex flavor from dried apricots, cumin, and other exotic and not-so-exotic ingredients. Serve it over cooked couscous for a satisfying meal.

1½ pounds chuck, cut into chunks

2 sweet potatoes (about 1 pound), cut into 1-inch cubes

1 (28-ounce) can whole peeled tomatoes

1 red onion, cut into wedges

½ cup dried apricots

2 teaspoons ground cumin

2 teaspoons ground ginger

½ teaspoon ground cinnamon

½ teaspoon cayenne

1 teaspoon kosher salt

Combine all the ingredients in a large bowl. To freeze before cooking, skip ahead to the storage instructions.

To cook, transfer the meat mixture to a slow cooker and add ½ cup water. Cover and cook on high for 6 to 8 hours, until the meat is very tender. Serve hot, or cool to room temperature before storing.

TO REFRIGERATE: Let the cooked dish come to room temperature, and then store, covered, in the refrigerator for up to three days. Reheat the cooked dish in a covered saucepan over medium heat, stirring occasionally, until heated through, about 10 minutes.

TO FREEZE: To freeze before cooking, seal the meat mixture in a large, resealable bag, removing as much air as possible. Freeze for up to three months. To cook, thaw in the refrigerator for 24 hours or in a bowl of water for up to an hour, changing the water once. Transfer the meat mixture to a slow cooker, add ½ cup water, cover, and cook for 6 to 8 hours on high, until the meat is very tender.

The dish can also be frozen after cooking. Let it come to room temperature, then transfer it to a large, resealable plastic bag or six individual freezer containers. Freeze for up to three months. Reheat from frozen in a covered saucepan set over medium heat. Cook, stirring occasionally, for 20 to 30 minutes, until heated through.

GLUTEN-FREE

DAIRY-FREE

SLOW-COOKED SHORT RIBS WITH CARROTS AND MUSHROOMS

SERVES 6 • PREP TIME: 10 MINUTES • COOK TIME: 8 HOURS

Cooking this dish in the slow cooker makes preparation incredibly easy. It's great for a weeknight family dinner, but the short ribs make it special enough to serve to company, too. Serve with a simple green salad and crusty bread for dipping into the flavorful sauce.

6 carrots, cut into 2-inch pieces

12 ounces mushrooms, diced

1 onion, diced

3 pounds beef short ribs

1 teaspoon kosher salt

1 teaspoon freshly ground black pepper

1 tablespoon garlic powder

6 cups beef broth

1 tablespoon cornstarch

To freeze before cooking, skip ahead to the storage instructions below.

To cook, put the carrots, mushrooms, and onion in the slow cooker. Rub the short ribs all over with the salt, pepper, and garlic powder, and place them on top of the vegetables in the slow cooker. Add the broth. Cover and cook on high for about 8 hours, until the meat is very tender.

Just before serving, scoop ½ cup of liquid from the slow cooker and whisk the cornstarch into it. Return the mixture to the slow cooker, and stir until the sauce thickens. Serve hot.

PALEO

DAIRY-FREE

GLUTEN-FREE: Use gluten-free beef broth.

TIP: For added flavor, replace up to two cups of the broth with dry red wine.

TO REFRIGERATE: To refrigerate before cooking, rub the short ribs all over with salt, pepper, and garlic powder, place in a large, resealable plastic bag, and add the carrots, mushrooms, and onion on top. Seal the bag and refrigerate for up to 24 hours. To cook, transfer the contents of the bag to the slow cooker, add the broth, cover, and cook on high for about 8 hours, until the meat is very tender. Follow the instructions above to thicken the sauce. Refrigerate the cooked dish for up to three days, and reheat on the stovetop or in the microwave.

TO FREEZE: To freeze the uncooked dish, rub the short ribs all over with salt, pepper, and garlic powder, place in a large, resealable plastic bag, and add the carrots, mushrooms, and onion on top. Seal the bag and freeze for up to three months. Make a note on the bag that you'll need six cups of beef broth and one tablespoon of cornstarch to cook the dish. To cook, thaw in the refrigerator for at least 24 hours, then transfer the contents of the bag to the slow cooker. Add the broth, cover, and cook on high for about 8 hours, until the meat is very tender. Follow the instructions above to thicken the sauce.

The cooked dish can be frozen for up to three months, as well. Thaw in the refrigerator or microwave, and reheat on the stovetop or in the microwave.

SPICY SWEET POTATO FRIES (PAGE 150)

chapter nine

SNACKS AND SIDES

FRUIT-AND-NUT FROZEN YOGURT BITES

MAKES 24 BITES • PREP TIME: 5 MINUTES • FREEZE TIME: 2 HOURS

These sweet bites are full of healthy ingredients but taste like an indulgent treat. They're perfect for an after-school snack or dessert on a warm day. And it's simple to vary this recipe to suit your taste or whatever ingredients you have on hand; just substitute different fruits, nuts, or yogurt flavors.

2 cups vanilla Greek yogurt
¾ cup chopped strawberries
¾ cup chopped banana
½ cup chopped almonds
¾ cup granola

In a medium bowl, stir together all the ingredients.

Line a 9-by-13-inch baking dish with aluminum foil, and pour the yogurt mixture into the pan, spreading it out into an even layer with a rubber spatula.

Cover the dish tightly with plastic wrap and freeze at least two hours, until frozen solid. Remove the baking dish from the freezer, lift the frozen yogurt out of the dish with the plastic wrap lining, and cut into 2-by-2-inch squares. Store in a large, resealable plastic bag in the freezer for up to three months.

GLUTEN-FREE: Use gluten-free granola.

TIP: You can also make these in silicone mini-muffin cups. Arrange the cups on a baking sheet before filling for easy transfer in and out of the freezer. Once they're frozen, pop the bites out of the silicone molds and store them in a large, resealable plastic bag in the freezer.

TO FREEZE: These bites will keep in the freezer for three months.

VEGETARIAN

COCONUT-ALMOND ENERGY BITES WITH CHOCOLATE CHIPS

MAKES ABOUT 36 BITES • PREP TIME: 15 MINUTES • COOK TIME: NONE

These sweet, no-bake bites can be eaten at room temperature, packed into a lunch box, or enjoyed as a frozen treat. They're loaded with protein, carbs, and fiber, so they'll fill you up and keep you satisfied. Vary the ingredients to suit your taste.

2 cups old-fashioned rolled oats
1 cup almond butter
⅔ cup honey
2 cups unsweetened flaked coconut
1 cup ground flaxseed
1 cup mini chocolate chips
2 teaspoons vanilla extract

In a large bowl, stir together all the ingredients until well combined. Roll the mixture into 1½-inch balls and arrange them in a single layer on a large, rimmed baking sheet.

GLUTEN-FREE: Use gluten-free oats.

TO REFRIGERATE: Cover the balls with plastic wrap and refrigerate for up to three days. Serve cold or bring to room temperature.

TO FREEZE: Cover the baking sheet with plastic wrap and freeze until the balls are frozen solid, at least 2 hours. Transfer the balls to a large, resealable plastic bag, and store in the freezer for up to three months. To serve, thaw the balls at room temperature for about 30 minutes, or warm them in the microwave for 20 to 30 seconds. They can also be eaten frozen.

VEGETARIAN

WHOLE-WHEAT BANANA– PEANUT BUTTER TOASTER PASTRIES

MAKES 8 PASTRIES • PREP TIME: 20 MINUTES, PLUS 30 MINUTES TO CHILL
THE PASTRIES • COOK TIME: 30 MINUTES

Made with whole-wheat flour and filled with bananas, peanut butter, and honey, these are a lot healthier than anything you'll buy in the store. Served warm from the toaster with a tall glass of cold milk, they always hit the spot. The crust is easy to make, but you can cut your prep time way down by using a good store-bought whole-wheat pie crust.

2 ¼ cups whole-wheat flour, plus extra for rolling out the dough

½ teaspoon fine sea salt

1 cup (2 sticks) cold, unsalted butter, cut into small pieces

⅓ to ½ cup ice water, divided

1 egg beaten with a splash of water

¾ cup peanut butter

2 tablespoons honey

2 ripe bananas, halved crosswise and cut into ¼-inch-thick slices

1 egg whisked with a teaspoon of water

Line a large, rimmed baking sheet with parchment paper.

In a food processor, combine the flour and salt, and pulse to mix. Add the butter to the flour in the food processor, and process just until the mixture resembles a coarse meal. With the motor running, add ⅓ cup of water and process just until the mixture comes together in a ball. If the mixture is too dry to form a ball, add additional ice water 1 or 2 teaspoons at a time.

Transfer the dough to a lightly floured board, sprinkle the top with a little bit of additional flour, and use a rolling pin to roll the dough out to a large rectangle about ⅛ inch thick. With a sharp knife, cut the dough into 16 rectangles of equal size. Arrange half the pieces on the prepared baking sheet.

In a small bowl, stir together the peanut butter and honey until well combined. Place about 1½ tablespoons of the peanut-butter mixture on top of each dough rectangle on the baking sheet, pressing it down with the back of the spoon so that it spreads out a bit. Top each dollop of peanut butter with 2 slices of banana. Finally, top with the remaining dough rectangles, and use a fork to crimp and seal the edge all the way around. Prick each pastry a couple of times with the fork to make holes for steam to escape while baking. Brush the tops with the egg wash. To freeze before baking, skip ahead to the freezing instructions.

THE HEALTHY MAKE-AHEAD COOKBOOK

Transfer the baking sheet to the refrigerator and chill the pastries for about 30 minutes.

Preheat the oven to 350°F.

Bake the pastries for 20 to 25 minutes, until lightly browned and crisp on top, then transfer to a cooling rack to cool. Serve warm. Pastries can be stored in an airtight container at room temperature for up to three days.

TIP: To create a PB&J version, swap out the honey for fruit preserves, jam, or jelly.

TO REFRIGERATE: Wrap the baked pastries and store them in the refrigerator for up to six days. To reheat, pop the pastries in the toaster.

TO FREEZE: Let the baked pastries cool to room temperature, then freeze on the baking sheet until frozen solid, at least 2 hours. Transfer the frozen pastries to a large, resealable plastic bag and keep in the freezer for up to three months. To reheat, pop the frozen pastries in the toaster.

The uncooked pastries can also be frozen on the baking sheet, transferred to a large, resealable plastic bag, and kept frozen for up to three months. To cook, preheat the oven to 350°F and arrange the frozen pastries on a baking sheet. Bake for 35 to 40 minutes, until lightly browned and crisp.

HONEY-NUT SNACK SQUARES

These nut-filled snack bars are loaded with protein, fiber, vitamins, and minerals, making them an all-around wholesome snack. Take them along on your next hike, pack them in a lunch box, or just keep them around for midafternoon noshing.

2 cups chopped nuts (such as cashews, almonds, pecans, and/or walnuts)
½ cup shredded unsweetened coconut
1 teaspoon vanilla extract
½ teaspoon fine sea salt
½ teaspoon cinnamon
½ cup plus 1 tablespoon honey

Preheat the oven to 350°F.

Line an 8-by-8-inch baking dish with parchment paper.

In a large bowl, stir together the nuts, coconut, vanilla, salt, and cinnamon. Add the honey, and stir with a fork to mix well.

Transfer the mixture to the prepared baking dish and spread it out into an even layer, pressing down so that the mixture is packed down and fills the entire bottom of the baking dish. Moisten your hands with a bit of cooking oil to keep the mixture from sticking to them as you do this. Bake in the preheated oven for 20 minutes.

Remove the pan from the oven, and set it on a cooling rack to cool for about 30 minutes. Lift the bars out of the pan using the parchment paper flaps. Invert the bars onto a cutting board and peel the parchment paper off. Cool to room temperature and cut into 2-inch squares. Serve at room temperature.

TO STORE: Wrap the squares individually in parchment paper and store in an airtight container at room temperature for up to a week.

TO FREEZE: Wrap the squares individually in parchment paper and store in a large, resealable plastic bag in the freezer for up to three months. Thaw at room temperature overnight.

PALEO

VEGETARIAN

GLUTEN-FREE

DAIRY-FREE

WHOLE-WHEAT ZUCCHINI MUFFINS

MAKES 12 MUFFINS • PREP TIME: 10 MINUTES • COOK TIME: 25 MINUTES

These healthy muffins are sweetened with both maple syrup and mashed banana. Serve them for breakfast or as an afternoon snack, and pat yourself on the back for not only using whole-grain flour but also sneaking in a green vegetable.

¼ cup cooking oil, plus extra for muffin tin

2 cups grated fresh zucchini

½ cup mashed banana (about 1 medium banana)

½ cup maple syrup

1 teaspoon vanilla extract

2 large eggs

1 teaspoon cinnamon

1 teaspoon baking soda

1 teaspoon baking powder

½ teaspoon fine sea salt

1⅔ cups white whole-wheat flour

Preheat the oven to 375°F.

Lightly oil a 12-cup muffin tin.

Wrap the zucchini in a towel and squeeze it to remove as much water as possible.

In a large mixing bowl or in the bowl of a stand mixer, combine the banana, maple syrup, oil, and vanilla, and beat until smooth. Add the eggs and beat to incorporate. Add the cinnamon, baking soda, baking powder, and salt, and beat to mix. Add the flour and beat on low speed just until the flour is fully incorporated. Gently stir in the zucchini.

Scoop the batter into the prepared muffin tin, filling each well about three-quarters full. Bake in the preheated oven for 22 to 24 minutes, or until a toothpick inserted in the middle of a muffin comes out clean. Place the muffin tin on a wire rack to cool for 5 minutes, then lift the muffins out of the tin, and let them cool completely on the rack. Serve warm or at room temperature.

TIP: For a special treat, stir in one cup of mini semisweet chocolate chips along with the grated zucchini.

TO STORE: The muffins can be stored in an airtight container lined with paper towels for up to a week. Place a double layer of paper towels on the bottom of the container, arranging the muffins on them in a single layer. Place another double layer of paper towels on top, fit the lid onto the container, and store at room temperature.

TO FREEZE: Wrap the muffins individually in plastic wrap and store in a large, resealable plastic bag in the freezer for up to three months. To serve, thaw completely at room temperature or gently in the microwave.

VEGETARIAN

DAIRY-FREE

SWEET POTATO PECAN MUFFINS

Even people who shy away from sweet potatoes are bound to love these moist, flavorful, maple syrup-sweetened muffins. Serve them for breakfast, as a snack, or even as a side to roast turkey or ham.

2 tablespoons cooking oil, plus extra for oiling tin

2 cups whole-wheat pastry flour

¼ teaspoon fine sea salt

2 teaspoons baking powder

½ teaspoon cinnamon

½ cup maple syrup

1 large egg

¾ cup mashed sweet potatoes

1 cup milk

1 teaspoon vanilla extract

⅔ cup chopped pecans

Preheat the oven to 375°F.

Lightly oil a muffin tin.

In a large bowl, stir together the flour, salt, baking powder, and cinnamon.

In a separate mixing bowl, combine the maple syrup, egg, oil, sweet potatoes, milk, and vanilla, and stir to mix well.

Add the wet ingredients to the dry ingredients, and stir to mix well. Stir in the pecans. Scoop the batter into the muffin tin.

Bake for 15 to 20 minutes, until a toothpick inserted into the center comes out clean. Set the muffin tin on a wire rack to cool for a few minutes before lifting out the muffins. Serve warm, or let the muffins cool completely on the wire rack.

TIP: If you don't have sweet potatoes on hand, you can substitute the same quantity of puréed pumpkin—either fresh or from a can—for an equally delicious result.

TO STORE: The muffins can be stored in an airtight container lined with paper towels for up to a week. Place a double layer of paper towels on the bottom of the container, and arrange the muffins on them in a single layer. Place another double layer of paper towels on top, fit the lid onto the container, and store at room temperature.

TO FREEZE: Wrap the muffins individually in plastic wrap, and store in a large, resealable plastic bag in the freezer for up to three months. To serve, thaw completely at room temperature or gently in the microwave.

VEGETARIAN

WHOLE-WHEAT PIZZA PINWHEELS

MAKES ABOUT 24 PINWHEELS • PREP TIME: 20 MINUTES, PLUS 90 MINUTES
TO LET THE DOUGH RISE • COOK TIME: 10 MINUTES

These are fun snacks to keep around for those times you suddenly have a bunch of hungry kids in the house after school or friends over to watch a game on TV. This is a simple version with just tomato sauce and cheese, but feel free to add any pizza toppings you like.

1 tablespoon instant yeast

1 cup warm water

1 tablespoon sugar

2 tablespoons olive oil

¾ cup all-purpose flour

1¾ cup whole-wheat flour

1¼ teaspoons kosher salt

1 cup Marinara Sauce (page 163) or jarred
    tomato sauce

2 cups shredded cheese

In the bowl of a stand mixer, whisk together the yeast, water, sugar, and oil. Let the mixture sit for about 10 minutes, until it becomes foamy.

Add the flours and salt. Knead using the dough hook until the mixture comes together in a smooth dough ball, 5 to 7 minutes. Add up to 2 tablespoons of water or additional flour if the dough is either too dry or too wet.

Cover with a clean dishtowel, and set in a warm spot on the countertop until it doubles in size, about 60 to 90 minutes.

Preheat the oven to 350°F and cover a baking sheet with parchment paper.

Divide the dough in half so you have two equally sized balls of dough. On a well-floured surface, roll or pat one of the dough balls out into a large rectangle about ¼ inch thick. Spread half the pizza sauce evenly over the dough and sprinkle half the cheese over the top. Starting from one of the long sides, roll the dough into a log. Slice into 1-inch pieces, and arrange them cut-side down on the prepared baking sheet. Repeat with the second ball of dough and the remaining sauce and cheese.

Bake in the preheated oven for about 10 minutes, until the tops are golden brown. Allow to cool on the baking sheet for a few minutes before serving.

TIP: If you don't have a stand mixer, mix the dough in a large mixing bowl with a wooden spoon and knead it by hand for about 10 minutes.

TO REFRIGERATE: Cover and refrigerate the pinwheels for up to five days. To reheat, bake them in a 350°F oven (on a baking sheet or pizza stone) for 6 to 8 minutes.

TO FREEZE: Wrap the pinwheels in plastic wrap and store in the freezer for up to three months. To serve, reheat from frozen in a 350°F oven (on a baking sheet or pizza stone) for about 20 minutes, or thaw in the refrigerator overnight and reheat in a 350°F oven for 6 to 8 minutes.

VEGETARIAN

These refried beans are slow cooked, along with onion and spices, until they're meltingly tender, then mashed to achieve that perfect chunky-smooth texture. Serve alongside tacos or enchiladas, or use as a filling for burritos.

1 pound dried pinto beans, soaked in water
    overnight and drained
1 onion, shredded
4 garlic cloves, minced
1 tablespoon ground cumin
2 teaspoons kosher salt
½ teaspoon cayenne

Place the soaked beans in the slow cooker along with the onion, garlic, cumin, salt, and cayenne. Add enough water to cover the beans by about 1 inch (about 7 or 8 cups of water). Cover and cook on high for 8 to 10 hours, until the beans are very tender. Strain the excess liquid from the beans, reserving the liquid.

Using a potato masher, mash the beans until they are mostly smooth but with some chunks of bean still remaining. Add some of the reserved cooking liquid to the beans to achieve the desired consistency. Serve hot, or cool to room temperature before storing.

TIP: Never cook dried beans in a slow cooker without first soaking them overnight, but if you forgot to soak them, don't fret! You can "quick soak" beans in an hour. Put the beans in a pot, and cover with about 2 inches of water. Bring to a boil and cook for about a minute. Remove from the heat, cover, let soak for one hour, and drain.

TO REFRIGERATE: Store the beans, covered, in the refrigerator for up to five days. Reheat in a saucepan on the stovetop or in the microwave.

TO FREEZE: Transfer the beans to a few small, resealable plastic bags or one large one. Remove as much air as possible, seal, and freeze for up to three months. To serve, thaw in the refrigerator overnight, in a bowl of cold water for up to an hour, or in the microwave. Reheat in a saucepan on the stovetop or in the microwave.

VEGAN

GLUTEN-FREE

RICH BAKED BEANS WITH BACON AND MOLASSES

Canned baked beans are pretty darn tasty, but with just a little effort you can make something even more delectable without any unwanted—and totally unnecessary—additives like high-fructose corn syrup or preservatives. This recipe makes the perfect side for burgers or barbecue.

8 slices bacon, chopped

1 onion, chopped

2 teaspoons chili powder

1 teaspoon kosher salt

1 pound dried pinto beans, soaked in water overnight and drained

4 cups water

1 cup ketchup

½ cup molasses

¼ cup (packed) light brown sugar

2 tablespoons apple cider vinegar

1 tablespoon Dijon mustard

Preheat the oven to 325°F.

Heat a Dutch oven or other oven-safe pot with a lid over medium heat, and cook the bacon for about 3 minutes. Raise the heat to high, add the onion, and cook, stirring, for about 5 minutes, until the bacon is crisp and the onions are soft. Add the chili powder and salt, and cook, stirring, for 1 minute.

Stir in the beans, water, ketchup, molasses, brown sugar, vinegar, and mustard. Bring to a simmer, cover, and transfer the pot to the preheated oven. Cook for 5 hours, stirring every couple of hours and adding water if the mixture looks too dry. Serve hot, or cool to room temperature before storing.

TIP: The dry heat of the oven helps to infuse the beans with intense flavor, but you could also cook them in a slow cooker, if necessary. Cook the bacon and onions as directed above, then mix everything in the slow cooker, cover, and cook on high for 8 to 10 hours.

TO REFRIGERATE: Store the cooked beans, covered, in the refrigerator for up to five days. Reheat on the stovetop or in the microwave.

TO FREEZE: Divide the beans into several small, resealable plastic bags, or put them in one large bag. Remove as much air as possible, seal, and freeze flat. To serve, thaw the beans in the refrigerator overnight, in a bowl of cold water, or in the microwave. Reheat on the stovetop or in the microwave.

GLUTEN-FREE

DAIRY-FREE

SPICY SWEET POTATO FRIES

Sweet potatoes are one of the most nutritious vegetables around, and baking these "fries" in the oven keeps them healthy. Serve as a snack with ketchup, salsa, or any of your favorite dipping sauces, or as a side to burgers, barbecue, or sandwiches.

2 large sweet potatoes, peeled and cut into fry-shaped pieces

Cooking oil spray

4 teaspoons cornstarch, divided

2 tablespoons cooking oil, divided

½ teaspoon kosher salt, plus extra for seasoning, divided

¼ to ½ teaspoon ground chipotle, divided

Place the cut sweet potatoes in a large bowl and cover them with cold water. Let soak for at least 1 hour or as long as overnight. Drain, rinse, and pat dry.

Preheat the oven to 425°F.

Line two baking sheets with aluminum foil and spray them lightly with cooking oil spray.

In a large plastic bag, combine half of the sweet potatoes with 2 teaspoons of cornstarch. Close up the bag and shake to coat the fries with the cornstarch. Empty the bag into a large bowl and toss with 1 tablespoon of oil, ¼ teaspoon of salt, and ⅛ to ¼ teaspoon of the chipotle. Transfer the fries to one of the prepared baking sheets and spread them out into a single layer.

Repeat with the rest of the fries and the remaining 2 teaspoons of cornstarch, 1 tablespoon of oil, ¼ teaspoon of salt, and ⅛ to ¼ teaspoon of chipotle. Arrange these fries on the second prepared baking sheet.

Bake both pans of sweet potato fries in the oven for 15 minutes. Use a spatula to flip the fries over, then switch the positions of the two baking sheets, and bake for another 10 to 15 minutes, until the fries are browned and cooked through.

Turn the oven off but leave the fries inside. Prop the oven door open halfway, and let the fries cool for about 10 minutes. (This will help them crisp up.) Sprinkle generously with salt and serve warm, or let cool to room temperature before storing.

TO REFRIGERATE: The fries can be refrigerated, covered, for up to five days. To reheat, place them on an oiled baking sheet in a 400°F oven for 15 to 20 minutes.

TO FREEZE: Freeze the fries on baking sheets until frozen solid, then transfer to resealable plastic bags. To serve, reheat the frozen fries on an oiled baking sheet in a 400°F oven for 20 to 25 minutes.

PALEO

VEGAN

GLUTEN-FREE

DAIRY-FREE

MASHED SWEET POTATO CUPS

These twice-baked, mashed sweet potatoes freeze and reheat particularly well, maintaining their full flavor. While I usually serve them with roasted or grilled meats, they also make a delicious snack or even a tasty quick breakfast.

2 large sweet potatoes or yams, cut crosswise into
  2½-to-3-inch-thick rounds
1 tablespoon olive oil
⅓ cup sour cream
2 teaspoons freshly squeezed lime juice
½ teaspoon kosher salt
½ teaspoon ground cumin
½ teaspoon chili powder

Preheat the oven to 400°F.

Rub the sweet potato pieces all over with the olive oil, and arrange them cut-side down on a large baking sheet. Bake in the preheated oven for about 45 minutes, turning them over once midway, until very tender. Remove from the oven and let cool until you can handle them, leaving the oven on if you plan to cook and serve them right away.

Scoop out the flesh of the sweet potato pieces using a small spoon, leaving about ¼ inch of flesh all the way around to make a bowl or cup. Place the scooped-out flesh into a bowl, and arrange the hollowed-out cups on the baking sheet. To refrigerate or freeze, skip ahead to the storage instructions.

Add the sour cream, lime juice, salt, cumin, and chili powder to the sweet potato flesh in the bowl, and stir to mix well. Spoon the mixture into the cups on the baking sheet, filling them equally. Return the baking sheet to the preheated oven, and bake for about 25 minutes, until the tops are beginning to brown and the filling is heated through. Serve hot.

TIP: Before baking, try topping each filled sweet potato cup with a tablespoon or two of shredded cheese.

TO REFRIGERATE: Cover and refrigerate for up to three days. To serve, bake in a 400°F oven for about 25 minutes, until the tops are beginning to brown and the filling is heated through.

TO FREEZE: Cover the baking sheet with plastic wrap and freeze until the sweet potato cups are frozen solid. Wrap individually in plastic wrap or transfer to a large, resealable plastic bag, and keep frozen for up to three months. To serve, thaw in the refrigerator overnight or in the microwave, and bake in a 400°F oven for about 25 minutes, until the tops are beginning to brown and the filling is heated through.

VEGETARIAN

GLUTEN-FREE

TANGY COLESLAW

Who would've guessed you could freeze coleslaw? But it's true. Not only can you freeze it, but the result, after thawing, is perfectly crisp and fresh. Serve this slaw as a topping for Slow Cooker Pulled Pork sandwiches (page 123) or alongside barbecue, burgers, Crispy Baked Fish Sticks (page 97), or Oven-Fried Chicken (page 108).

1¼ cups sugar

¾ cup apple-cider vinegar

1½ pounds finely shredded cabbage

1 large carrot, peeled and shredded

1 red bell pepper, diced

1 teaspoon celery salt

1 teaspoon mustard seeds

½ teaspoon freshly ground black pepper

In a small saucepan, stir together the sugar and vinegar, and bring to a boil over medium-high heat. Cook, stirring, until the sugar dissolves, for 2 to 3 minutes. Remove from the heat and let cool.

In a large bowl, toss together the cabbage, carrot, bell pepper, celery salt, mustard seeds, and pepper. Pour the vinegar-sugar mixture over the vegetables, and toss to mix well. Chill, covered, in the refrigerator for at least 2 hours, and serve cold.

TIP: To save time on prep, use bagged, shredded cabbage.

TO REFRIGERATE: Store covered in the refrigerator for up to three days. Serve cold.

TO FREEZE: Transfer the slaw to one large, resealable plastic bag or several small ones. Remove as much air as possible, seal, and freeze flat. Store in the freezer for up to three months. To serve, thaw the bag in the refrigerator overnight or in a bowl of water for up to an hour. Serve cold.

VEGAN

GLUTEN-FREE

DAIRY-FREE

ROSEMARY ROASTED VEGETABLES

SERVES 10 TO 12 • PREP TIME: 15 MINUTES • COOK TIME: 1 HOUR

A platter of roasted vegetables complements just about any meal, but it can take over an hour to get it cooked and on the table. I make a big batch and then freeze meal-size portions in resealable plastic bags to guarantee I've always got a healthy side on hand. Roasted vegetables also make excellent additions to burritos, scrambled eggs, or salads.

4 large beets, peeled and cut into cubes

6 Yukon gold potatoes, cut into wedges

2 red bell peppers, seeded and diced

2 carrots, peeled and cut into 2-inch-thick lengths

2 zucchini, cut into 2-inch-thick lengths

1 onion, halved and sliced

4 rosemary sprigs

¼ cup olive oil

1 teaspoon kosher salt

Preheat the oven to 425°F.

In a large baking dish or roasting pan, or on a large, rimmed baking sheet, toss together the beets, potatoes, bell peppers, carrots, zucchini, onion, and rosemary sprigs. Drizzle the olive oil over the top, and then toss to coat. Sprinkle with salt, and spread the vegetables out in a single layer.

Roast in the preheated oven for 45 to 60 minutes, until the vegetables are tender and nicely browned. Serve hot, or cool to room temperature before storing.

TIP: To ensure that the vegetables roast evenly, cut them into similarly sized pieces, spreading them out as much as possible on the pan.

TO REFRIGERATE: Store the roasted vegetables covered in the refrigerator for up to six days. They can be served cold, at room temperature, or reheated in the microwave.

TO FREEZE: Divide the vegetables into several resealable plastic bags. Remove as much air as possible, seal, and freeze flat for up to three months. To serve, thaw the bag(s) in the refrigerator overnight, in a bowl of water, or in the microwave. Serve cold, at room temperature, or reheated in the microwave.

VEGAN

GLUTEN-FREE

DAIRY-FREE

QUINOA PILAF WITH DRIED APRICOTS AND ALMONDS

With more protein than any other grain, quinoa is terrific for vegans and vegetarians. It also makes a great side for meat dishes. Quinoa comes in red, white, and black. You can use any color; just be sure to rinse it before cooking, because the natural saponins that coat quinoa can cause stomach upset. I love to serve it alongside grilled meats, or toss it into a salad.

1½ cups apple juice
1½ cups vegetable broth or chicken broth
1½ tablespoons olive oil
8 dried apricot halves, chopped
1½ cups quinoa, rinsed
½ teaspoon kosher salt
¼ cup toasted sliced almonds

In a medium saucepan, combine the apple juice, broth, oil, and apricots, and bring to a boil over medium-high heat. Stir in the quinoa and salt, and simmer, uncovered, for about 15 minutes.

Remove from the heat, cover, and let stand for 5 minutes. Stir in the almonds. Serve hot, or let cool to room temperature before storing.

GLUTEN-FREE: Use gluten-free broth.

VEGETARIAN/VEGAN: Use vegetable broth.

TO REFRIGERATE: Refrigerate the cooked quinoa, covered, for up to five days. To serve, reheat on the stovetop or in the microwave.

TO FREEZE: Transfer the quinoa to one large, resealable plastic bag or two small ones. Remove as much air as possible, seal, and freeze flat for up to three months. To serve, thaw the bag(s) in the refrigerator overnight, in a bowl of water, or in the microwave. Reheat in the microwave or on the stovetop.

DAIRY-FREE

GINGER BROWN RICE

Infused with the kick of fresh ginger, this brown rice side is a perfect accompaniment to just about any Asian-style grilled or stir-fried meat or vegetable dish. Try it with Spicy Orange Broccoli Shrimp Stir-Fry (page 88) or Stir-Fried Spicy Chicken with Green Beans (page 112).

3 cups long-grain brown rice

6 cups water

1 (1-inch) piece of ginger, peeled and cut into coins

1 teaspoon kosher salt

In a medium saucepan over medium heat, stir together the rice, water, ginger, and salt, and bring to a boil. Reduce the heat to low, cover, and simmer for 50 minutes.

Remove the pan from the heat, but leave the lid on. Let stand for 10 minutes, then remove the lid and fluff with a fork. Serve hot, or cool to room temperature before storing.

TIP: This dish can be turned into a great fried rice by stir-frying the cold, thawed rice with a bit of cooking oil and adding blanched carrots, frozen peas, scrambled eggs, and/or chopped, cooked meat or vegetables.

TO REFRIGERATE: Transfer the rice from the saucepan to a bowl or storage container, cover, and refrigerate for up to two days. To serve, reheat, covered, in the microwave, or reheat in a skillet with a bit of cooking oil.

TO FREEZE: Transfer the rice to one large or several smaller resealable plastic bags. Remove as much air as possible, seal, and freeze flat for up to three months. To serve, thaw the bag in the refrigerator overnight or in a bowl of cold water. Reheat, covered, in the microwave, or in a skillet with a bit of cooking oil.

VEGAN

GLUTEN-FREE

DAIRY-FREE

FRESH BASIL PESTO (PAGE 166)

chapter ten

KITCHEN STAPLES

HERB-AND-GARLIC BUTTER

MAKES ½ CUP • PREP TIME: 5 MINUTES • COOK TIME: NONE

Compound butter—any butter with herbs, spices, or aromatics blended into it—makes an instant flavorful sauce for grilled or roasted meat, fish, or vegetables. Freeze it in a log shape, and then any time you need a little something to liven up a meal, slice off a pat (or a few), place it on top of your hot food, and watch it melt. It can also be used as a spread on muffins, rolls, or toast.

1 small garlic clove

½ small shallot

½ cup chopped flat-leaf parsley

½ cup (1 stick) unsalted butter, at room
    temperature

2 tablespoons freshly squeezed lemon juice

1 teaspoon kosher salt

¼ teaspoon freshly ground black pepper

Chop the garlic and shallot in a food processor. Add the parsley, and pulse until finely minced. Add the butter, lemon juice, salt, and pepper, and process until smooth.

Using a rubber spatula, scrape the butter mixture out of the food processor onto a piece of plastic wrap. Form the butter into a log about 2 inches in diameter, and wrap it tightly in the plastic wrap.

TIP: You can use any herbs you like—cilantro, chives, basil, or mint, for example. You can also add other flavorings such as lemon, lime, or orange zest, dried chilies, or ground spices.

TO REFRIGERATE: Compound butter can be stored in the refrigerator for up to a week. Serve cold, or for soft, spreadable butter, let it come to room temperature before serving.

TO FREEZE: Store in the freezer for up to three months. Use it straight out of the freezer, without thawing, or, for soft, spreadable butter, let it come to room temperature before serving.

VEGETARIAN

GLUTEN-FREE

HOMEMADE TACO SEASONING MIX

MAKES ABOUT 1¼ CUPS • PREP TIME: 5 MINUTES • COOK TIME: NONE

Taco seasoning packets are convenient for turning plain ground meat into a flavorful taco filling. This homemade version gives you the same ability, but without any unnatural additives. Add about 2 tablespoons of the seasoning mix to a pound of cooked ground meat, along with a bit of broth or water, and simmer until the sauce thickens. Beyond tacos, I also like to use this seasoning mix for spicing up a pot of beans, flavoring dips and spreads, or as a spice rub for grilled or roasted meats.

½ cup chili powder

¼ cup plus 2 tablespoons ground cumin

2 tablespoons paprika

2 tablespoons salt

1 tablespoon garlic powder

1 tablespoon onion powder

1 tablespoon dried oregano

1 tablespoon black pepper

2 teaspoons cayenne

In a small bowl, combine all the ingredients, and stir to mix.

TO STORE: Transfer the spice mixture to a glass jar with a lid and seal tightly. Store at room temperature for up to three months.

TO FREEZE: Transfer the spice mixture to a pint-size resealable plastic bag, remove as much air as possible, and seal. Store in the freezer indefinitely.

SWEET-SPICY BARBECUE SAUCE

Homemade barbecue sauce is the best, so why not make a large batch and freeze it? Use it on grilled chicken, ribs, or steak, dip Homemade Crunchy Chicken Tenders (page 107) in it, or mix it with Slow Cooker Pulled Pork (page 123) for pulled pork sandwiches.

2 onions

4 garlic cloves

2 tablespoons olive oil

3 (14.5-ounce) cans tomato sauce

1 cup (packed) dark brown sugar

½ cup apple cider vinegar

¼ cup Worcestershire sauce

1 teaspoon cayenne

1 teaspoon smoked paprika or ground chipotle

In a food processor, process the onion and garlic to a smooth purée.

Heat the oil in a heavy saucepan over medium-high heat. Add the onion-and-garlic mixture and cook, stirring, for about 5 minutes, until it begins to brown. Stir in the tomato sauce, sugar, vinegar, Worcestershire sauce, cayenne, and smoked paprika or chipotle, and bring to a boil.

Lower the heat and simmer, stirring occasionally, for about 45 minutes, until the sauce thickens and begins to darken. Remove from the heat. Serve immediately, or let cool to room temperature before storing.

GLUTEN-FREE: Use gluten-free Worcestershire sauce.

VEGETARIAN/VEGAN: Look for Worcestershire sauce without anchovies.

TO REFRIGERATE: Transfer the sauce to a large glass jar or other storage container, cover, and refrigerate for up to a week. Reheat in a saucepan on the stovetop, or serve at room temperature.

TO FREEZE: Divide the sauce into meal-size portions and transfer them to lidded freezer containers (not resealable plastic bags). I like to use canning jars because they can be used to reheat the sauce as well. Just be sure to leave plenty of headspace to allow for the fact that the sauce will expand as it freezes. To serve, thaw in the refrigerator overnight or in the microwave, or place the jar or other container in a bowl or saucepan of hot water. Serve warm or at room temperature.

DAIRY-FREE

RED CHILE SAUCE

Ladled over Chicken-and-Spinach Enchiladas (page 114), this rich, spicy sauce is what makes the dish a favorite. But you can also use it for so much more! Try it on Mexican classics like burritos and tamales, stirred into beans, or as a sauce for roasted or grilled meats or seafood.

6 dried ancho chiles, stemmed and seeded

2 large garlic cloves

1 teaspoon kosher salt

1 teaspoon ground cumin

1 teaspoon dried oregano

2 tablespoons cooking oil

2 tablespoons all-purpose flour

1 cup tomato sauce

In a medium saucepan, cover the chiles with water, and bring to a boil over medium-high heat. Cook for about 1 minute, then remove from the heat and let stand for about 10 minutes, until softened. Using a slotted spoon, transfer the chiles to a blender, reserving the soaking liquid.

Add the garlic, salt, cumin, oregano, and 1½ cups of the soaking liquid to the blender. Blend until smooth, about 2 minutes.

Discard any remaining soaking liquid and seeds left in the saucepan, and add the oil. Heat over medium-high heat, then whisk in the flour and reduce the heat to medium.

Cook, whisking constantly, for about 5 minutes, until the flour begins to darken and give off a nutty aroma.

Transfer the chile mixture from the blender to the saucepan, along with the tomato sauce, and bring to a simmer. Cook, stirring occasionally, for about 15 minutes, until the sauce thickens. Serve immediately, or let cool to room temperature before storing.

TIP: You can buy dried ancho chiles in many supermarkets, Latin markets, or online. If you don't have them, substitute three tablespoons of ground ancho chile powder (not generic "chili powder"). If you don't have that, use three tablespoons of paprika, and add cayenne to achieve the spice level you desire.

TO REFRIGERATE: Store, covered, in the refrigerator for up to a week.

TO FREEZE: Transfer the sauce to a jar or other freezer-safe container with a lid. (Remember to leave a bit of headspace, because it'll expand as it freezes.) The sauce will keep in the freezer for up to three months. To serve, thaw in the refrigerator overnight, then reheat in the microwave or in a saucepan on the stovetop.

VEGAN

DAIRY-FREE

PINEAPPLE SALSA

This fresh-tasting tropical fruit salsa contains a healthy kick. Pineapple holds up much better to freezing than fresh tomatoes, which can get watery and lose their flavor. Use this salsa on tacos—especially Fish Tacos (page 93)—on quesadillas, or on burritos, or as a dip for chips.

2 cups diced pineapple
½ red onion, diced
Juice of 1 lime
1 to 2 jalapeño peppers, seeded and diced
2 tablespoons minced cilantro
½ teaspoon kosher salt

In a medium bowl, stir together all of the ingredients.

To serve, cover and refrigerate for one hour, and serve chilled.

TIP: To experiment with a different flavor, you can substitute the same amount of diced mango for the pineapple, or even combine the two.

TO REFRIGERATE: Cover and refrigerate for up to a week. Serve chilled.

TO FREEZE: Transfer the salsa to one medium, resealable plastic bag or two small ones. Remove as much air as possible, seal, and freeze flat for up to three months. To serve, thaw the bag in the refrigerator overnight or in a bowl of water for up to an hour.

PALEO

VEGAN

GLUTEN-FREE

DAIRY-FREE

MARINARA SAUCE

MAKES ABOUT 3 ½ CUPS • PREP TIME: 5 MINUTES • COOK TIME: 35 MINUTES

No store-bought pasta sauce tastes as good as one that's homemade. Make a double or triple batch of this quick-cooking sauce, and you'll always be prepared for a delicious spaghetti dinner. You can also use it as a sauce for fish or pizza.

1 onion, quartered
5 garlic cloves
2 tablespoons olive oil
1 (28-ounce) can tomato purée
1 tablespoon Italian seasoning
1 teaspoon kosher salt
½ teaspoon freshly ground pepper

In a food processor, purée the onion and garlic together.

Heat the oil in a large saucepan or Dutch oven over medium heat. Add the onion-garlic mixture, cover, and cook for about 7 minutes, until the mixture becomes fragrant.

Stir in the tomato purée, Italian seasoning, salt, and pepper. Cover and cook for 25 minutes.

Serve hot, or let cool to room temperature before storing.

TO REFRIGERATE: Store, covered, in the refrigerator for up to a week. Reheat in a saucepan on the stovetop or in the microwave.

TO FREEZE: Transfer the sauce to one large, lidded container, or two or more smaller ones. Be sure to leave enough headspace for the sauce to expand as it freezes. Freeze for up to three months. To serve, thaw the container in the refrigerator overnight, in a bowl of water, or in the microwave. Reheat in the microwave or in a saucepan on the stovetop.

PALEO

VEGAN

GLUTEN-FREE

DAIRY-FREE

BOLOGNESE SAUCE

SERVES 8 TO 10 • PREP TIME: 10 MINUTES • COOK TIME: 2 HOURS, 15 MINUTES

This meaty sauce turns plain spaghetti into a hearty meal. Make a large batch and store it in meal-size portions in resealable plastic bags, then just pull one out for a quick meal at a moment's notice. Serve it over cooked pasta, topped with Parmesan cheese.

½ cup olive oil

2 carrots, shredded

1 large onion, diced

5 garlic cloves, minced

2 pounds lean ground beef

2 tablespoons dried oregano

¾ cup tomato paste

2 (28-ounce) cans whole tomatoes, drained

2 teaspoons kosher salt

1 teaspoon freshly ground black pepper

Heat the oil in a large saucepan or Dutch oven over medium heat. Add the carrots, onion, and garlic, and cook, stirring frequently, until soft, about 5 minutes. Add the beef and continue to cook, stirring and breaking up the meat with a spatula, until the meat is browned, about 5 minutes more.

Add the oregano and tomato paste, and cook, stirring, for 2 minutes. Stir in the tomatoes, breaking them up with a spatula. Stir in the salt and pepper, and bring to a boil.

Reduce the heat to medium-low and simmer for 1 to 2 hours, stirring occasionally. Serve hot, or let cool to room temperature before storing.

TO REFRIGERATE: Cover and refrigerate for up to three days. To serve, reheat in the microwave or in a saucepan on the stovetop.

TO FREEZE: Transfer to a large, resealable plastic bag or lidded freezer container (or several smaller ones). If using plastic bags, remove as much air as possible, seal, and freeze flat for up to three months. To serve, thaw the bag in the refrigerator overnight, in a bowl of water, or in the microwave. Reheat in a saucepan on the stovetop, or in the microwave.

PALEO

GLUTEN-FREE

DAIRY-FREE

SLOW COOKER CHICKEN BROTH

Whenever I cook a whole chicken, in either the oven or the slow cooker, I save the carcass to make broth. Once the meat is removed from the bones, I put the bones immediately into the slow cooker, add the other ingredients, and turn it on. When I wake up in the morning, I've got a big pot of broth ready for the freezer. When you make it yourself, feel free to add any other vegetable trimmings or herbs you like.

Chicken bones from 1 whole chicken
1 onion, quartered
2 celery ribs, cut into 3-inch pieces
2 carrots, cut into 3-inch pieces
1 tablespoon salt (optional)
Several whole black peppercorns

Place the bones, onion, celery, carrots, salt, and peppercorns in a 6-quart slow cooker. Fill the slow cooker all the way to the maximum fill line with water. Cover and cook on high for 12 hours or longer.

Once the broth is finished cooking, turn the slow cooker off, and remove the lid to let the broth cool down a bit. Strain the broth through a fine-meshed sieve into a large bowl.

Cover and refrigerate the broth for at least 6 hours, allowing the fat to rise to the top and solidify.

Skim the solidified fat off the top of the broth. The broth can be used immediately or stored.

TO REFRIGERATE: Cover the broth and refrigerate for up to three days.

TO FREEZE: Transfer the broth to four quart-size lidded jars or resealable plastic bags. (I prefer plastic bags since they can be frozen flat.) Freeze for up to three months. To use, thaw in the refrigerator overnight, in a bowl of cold water, in the microwave, or in a saucepan on the stovetop.

PALEO

GLUTEN-FREE

DAIRY-FREE

FRESH BASIL PESTO

Pesto made with fresh basil freezes beautifully, allowing you to enjoy its fresh taste any time of year. Use pesto as a pasta sauce or to flavor sauces, soups, or salad dressings. Or try it as a sandwich spread or a sauce for grilled meats. You can substitute different herbs for the basil (I love cilantro or mint pesto), as well as other nuts, like walnuts or almonds, for the pine nuts.

½ cup toasted pine nuts

2 garlic cloves

4 cups fresh basil

1 cup grated Parmesan cheese

Juice and zest of 1 lemon

1 teaspoon kosher salt

1 teaspoon freshly ground black pepper

1 cup olive oil

Preheat the oven to 350°F.

Spread the pine nuts on a baking sheet in a single layer. Bake in the preheated oven for 5 to 7 minutes, until lightly browned and fragrant.

In a food processor, chop the garlic. Add the basil and pulse until finely minced. Add the Parmesan, pine nuts, lemon juice and zest, salt, and pepper. Pulse until the mixture is finely chopped.

With the food processor running, add the olive oil in a thin, steady stream. Process until smooth.

TIP: Before freezing, top the pesto with a thin layer of olive oil (either in an ice cube tray or in jars; see freezing instructions below). If using an ice cube tray, cover with plastic wrap pressed directly onto the surface of the olive oil. These extra steps prevent the pesto from turning brown due to oxygen exposure.

TO REFRIGERATE: Transfer the pesto to a lidded container, and refrigerate for up to three days.

TO FREEZE: To freeze in small quantities for seasoning a sauce or topping grilled meat, spoon the pesto into an ice cube tray. Freeze until frozen solid, at least 2 hours. Transfer the frozen cubes to a resealable plastic bag for up to three months. Alternatively, pesto can be frozen in small, lidded jars. Half-cup (4-ounce) jars hold just enough for a typical pasta dinner. To serve, thaw in the refrigerator overnight or in the microwave, or add the frozen cubes to hot pasta or sauce. If you've frozen your pesto in jars, it can be thawed, in the jar, in a bowl of water.

VEGETARIAN

GLUTEN-FREE

SLOW COOKER CARAMELIZED ONIONS

Caramelizing onions is typically done by cooking them very slowly, stirring regularly over low heat until the onions turn golden brown and their sugars caramelize. This gives the onions a rich, savory flavor, but it's a time-consuming process. Using the slow cooker is a brilliant solution. Add caramelized onions to pasta dishes, sandwiches, wraps, or sauces.

4 large yellow onions, halved and thinly sliced
2 tablespoons unsalted butter, melted
2 tablespoons olive oil
1 teaspoon kosher salt
½ teaspoon freshly ground black pepper

In a 5-quart or larger slow cooker, stir together the onions, butter, olive oil, salt, and pepper. Cover and cook on low for 12 hours.

Serve immediately, or bring to room temperature before storing.

DAIRY-FREE/VEGAN: Use all olive oil instead of both olive oil and butter.

TIP: If you like your caramelized onions really concentrated and jam-like, after the 12 hours, set the lid of the slow cooker slightly ajar, and let cook for another 2 or 3 hours. This will allow liquid to evaporate and the flavors to concentrate even more.

TO REFRIGERATE: Using a slotted spoon, transfer the onions to a bowl, cover, and refrigerate for up to three days.

TO FREEZE: Using a slotted spoon, transfer the onions to a quart-size resealable plastic bag or four (1-cup) resealable plastic bags, and freeze for up to six months. To serve, defrost in the refrigerator overnight or in the microwave.

VEGETARIAN

GLUTEN-FREE

OATMEAL RAISIN COOKIES (PAGE 178)

chapter eleven

DESSERTS

VERY BLUEBERRY CRISP

SERVES 6 • PREP TIME: 10 MINUTES • COOK TIME: 1 HOUR

When it's blueberry season, there's no better way to use up the bounty than pouring a big pile of it in a baking dish, topping with a crispy oat-and-brown-sugar topping, and baking to sweet, syrupy perfection. During the rest of the year, you'll need to switch to frozen blueberries—but the result can be just as tasty.

½ cup plus 2 tablespoons unsalted butter, cut into small pieces, divided, plus extra for preparing the pan

6 cups fresh or frozen blueberries

⅓ cup granulated sugar

¼ cup plus 1 tablespoon all-purpose flour, divided

2 teaspoons cinnamon, divided

1 cup old-fashioned rolled oats

¼ cup brown sugar

Lightly coat a 9-inch-square baking dish with butter. (If planning to freeze, use a disposable aluminum cake pan with a lid.)

In a large bowl, stir together the blueberries, granulated sugar, ¼ cup of flour, 2 tablespoons of butter, and ½ teaspoon of cinnamon. Transfer the fruit mixture to the prepared pan.

In a separate medium bowl, combine the oats and brown sugar with the remaining tablespoon of flour, ½ cup of butter, and 1½ teaspoons of cinnamon. Mix the ingredients with a fork or your hands until the mixture is crumbly.

To cook, preheat the oven to 350°F.

Bake the crisp in the preheated oven for 50 to 60 minutes, until the topping is golden brown and the filling is bubbling.

TIP: For variety, substitute the same amount of another fruit, such as peaches, apples, blackberries, strawberries, nectarines, or a combination, depending on what you have on hand.

TO REFRIGERATE: Cover the pan containing the fruit mixture with plastic wrap, aluminum foil, or a lid. Transfer the topping mixture to a quart-size, resealable plastic bag. Store both the fruit and topping in the refrigerator for up to two days. To cook, preheat the oven to 350°F. Spread the topping on top of the fruit in an even layer. Bake in the preheated oven for 50 to 60 minutes, until the topping is golden brown and the filling is bubbling.

TO FREEZE: Spread the topping mixture on top of the fruit mixture in an even layer, cover with the pan lid or plastic wrap, and freeze for up to three months. To cook, preheat the oven to 350°F. Cover the pan with aluminum foil and bake from frozen for 45 minutes. Remove the cover and continue to bake for 25 to 30 minutes longer, until the topping is golden brown and the filling is bubbling.

VEGETARIAN

PUMPKIN PIE CUSTARD

The hardest part of making a pumpkin pie is the crust, but it's the flavorful filling we crave. Even for someone with a weakness for buttery, flaky pastry crust, I find this healthier version totally hits the spot. It's creamy and rich, full of the pumpkin and spice flavors we all enjoy in the fall.

Cooking oil (coconut, sunflower seed, etc.) for preparing the ramekins

2 whole large eggs

2 large egg yolks

¾ cup (packed) dark brown sugar

½ teaspoon fine sea salt

2 teaspoons cinnamon

1 teaspoon ground ginger

2 cups canned pumpkin purée

1½ cups (12 ounces) evaporated milk

Preheat the oven to 350°F.

Lightly oil 6 (6-ounce) ramekins and arrange them on a large baking sheet.

In a large bowl, beat the eggs, egg yolks, sugar, salt, cinnamon, and ginger. Add the pumpkin purée and evaporated milk, and beat to mix well.

Divide the pumpkin mixture equally among the prepared ramekins, and bake for about 30 minutes, until a knife inserted into the center of one of the custards comes out clean. Remove from the oven and set on a wire rack to cool completely. Serve at room temperature or store.

DAIRY-FREE: Substitute a nondairy milk alternative for the evaporated milk.

TO REFRIGERATE: Cover the ramekins with plastic wrap and refrigerate for up to three days. To serve, bring to room temperature by setting on the countertop for about 20 minutes before serving.

TO FREEZE: Cover the ramekins tightly with plastic wrap, pressing the plastic directly onto the surface of the custard. Freeze for up to three months. To serve, unwrap the custards and thaw them in the refrigerator for at least 4 hours. Bring to room temperature by setting them on the countertop for about 20 minutes before serving.

VEGETARIAN

GLUTEN-FREE

STRAWBERRY FROZEN YOGURT POPS

MAKES 6 ICE POPS • PREP TIME: 5 MINUTES, PLUS 20 MINUTES TO MACERATE FRUIT,
AND OVERNIGHT TO FREEZE • COOK TIME: NONE

Fresh fruit and yogurt make a healthy snack if ever there was one. Add a bit of sugar, freeze into ice pops, and you've got yourself a treat that makes everyone happy. Keep these refreshing frozen pops in your freezer all summer long.

1 pint fresh strawberries, trimmed and chopped
¼ cup sugar
1 teaspoon lemon juice
8 ounces full-fat plain yogurt

Put the strawberries in a medium bowl, add the sugar, and stir to combine. Let stand for about 15 minutes, stirring every few minutes, until the mixture becomes syrupy.

In a food processor, combine the strawberry and sugar mixture with the lemon juice, and pulse to purée the strawberries. Add the yogurt and pulse a few times, until just combined.

Transfer the mixture into 6 (3-ounce) ice-pop molds, and freeze overnight. Serve frozen.

DAIRY-FREE/VEGAN: Use nondairy yogurt.

TIP: Use any fruit or combination of fruits you like in this recipe. Substitute another type of berries (blueberries, blackberries, or raspberries) or another type of fruit altogether (peaches, plums, or nectarines), to name a few options.

TO FREEZE: The ice pops can be stored in the freezer for up to three months.

VEGETARIAN

GLUTEN-FREE

PEANUT BUTTER–FILLED BROWNIE CUPS

MAKES 24 BROWNIES • PREP TIME: 10 MINUTES • COOK TIME: 15 MINUTES

Chocolaty, rich, and filled with creamy, lightly sweetened peanut butter, these little brownie bites deliver big flavor. Serve them with a tall glass of milk as an afternoon snack, or with coffee as a grown-up, after-dinner dessert; they're equally irresistible any time of day.

½ cup plus 1 tablespoon melted coconut oil, divided, plus additional for preparing the muffin tin
½ cup whole-wheat flour
⅔ cup sugar
½ cup unsweetened cocoa powder
½ teaspoon baking powder
½ teaspoon fine sea salt
1 banana
2 teaspoons vanilla extract, divided
¼ cup creamy all-natural peanut butter
1 tablespoon maple syrup

Preheat the oven to 350°F.

Lightly coat a mini muffin tin with coconut oil.

In a medium bowl, stir the flour, sugar, cocoa powder, baking powder, and salt. In a separate large bowl, mash the banana. Add ½ cup of coconut oil and 1 teaspoon of vanilla, and stir to mix well.

Add the dry ingredients to the banana mixture, and stir to mix. Spoon the mixture into the prepared muffin tin, filling each cup to the top.

In a small bowl, combine the peanut butter, the remaining tablespoon of coconut oil, the maple syrup, and the remaining teaspoon of vanilla. Heat in the microwave for about 15 seconds and stir to mix well.

Drop a spoonful of the peanut-butter mixture in the center of each of each brownie.

Bake in the preheated oven for 15 minutes. Remove from the oven and let cool in the pan for 10 minutes. Transfer the brownies to a wire rack to cool completely.

TIP: Try hazelnut or almond butter instead of peanut butter for a flavor twist.

TO STORE: Store brownies in an airtight container at room temperature for up to a week.

TO FREEZE: Freeze brownies in a single layer on a baking sheet, then transfer to a large, resealable plastic bag. Brownies will last in the freezer for up to three months. To serve, thaw at room temperature overnight.

VEGAN

GLUTEN-FREE

CHOCOLATE-ALMOND MINI TEA CAKES

MAKES 15 TEA CAKES • PREP TIME: 10 MINUTES • COOK TIME: 15 MINUTES

Almond flour stands in for wheat flour in these delightful little cakes, giving them a distinctive texture. They're perfect with a cup of coffee or tea, and just the thing when you want something chocolaty and delicious, but not too heavy.

6 tablespoons unsalted butter, melted and cooled to room temperature, plus additional for preparing the muffin tin

1 cup almond flour

¾ cup powdered sugar

¼ cup unsweetened cocoa powder

⅛ teaspoon fine sea salt

2 large egg whites

¼ teaspoon almond or vanilla extract

Preheat the oven to 400°F.

Lightly coat a mini muffin tin with butter.

In a medium mixing bowl, whisk together the almond flour, powdered sugar, cocoa powder, and salt. Add the egg whites and almond or vanilla extract, and, while stirring, drizzle in the melted butter. Stir until the mixture is well combined and smooth, and the melted butter is completely incorporated. Spoon the batter into the molds, filling them three-quarters full.

Bake in the preheated oven for 10 to 15 minutes, until they puff up a bit. Remove from the oven and let cool completely in the muffin tin.

TIP: If you don't have almond flour, you can make your own by grinding almonds in a food processor until powdered.

TO STORE: These cakes can be stored at room temperature in an airtight container for up to a week.

TO FREEZE: Freeze the cakes on a baking sheet until frozen solid, then transfer to a large, resealable plastic bag. To serve, thaw at room temperature for several hours.

VEGETARIAN

GLUTEN-FREE

PB&J COOKIES

These simple thumbprint cookies pack all the comforting flavors of a peanut butter-and-jelly sandwich into a crunchy, sweet cookie. And they're pretty, too! They make a great addition to a holiday cookie platter, but are appropriate at any time of year.

½ cup (1 stick) unsalted butter, at room temperature
½ cup all-natural peanut butter
½ cup (packed) light brown sugar
½ cup granulated sugar
½ teaspoon fine sea salt
½ teaspoon vanilla extract
1 large egg, beaten
¾ cup whole-wheat flour
¾ cup all-purpose flour
⅓ cup berry jam or preserves

In a large bowl or in the bowl of a stand mixer, beat together the butter, peanut butter, brown sugar, and granulated sugar on medium-high speed until well mixed and creamy. Add the salt, vanilla, and egg, and beat to combine. Add the wheat flour and all-purpose flour, ½ cup at a time, beating on low speed after each addition, until fully incorporated.

Transfer the dough to a bowl or lidded storage container, cover, and refrigerate for 2 hours.

Preheat the oven to 350°F (if planning to bake right away), and line two large baking sheets with parchment paper.

Remove the dough from the refrigerator. To form the cookies, scoop out about a table-spoon of the dough and roll it between your palms to form a ball. Place each ball on the prepared baking sheets, leaving about 1 inch between them.

Press your thumb into the center of each ball to make an indentation, and add about ½ tea-spoon of jam or preserves into each one. To freeze, skip ahead to the storage instructions.

Bake in the preheated oven for about 12 minutes, until light golden brown. Transfer the cookies to a wire rack to cool before serving.

TIP: Use any type of fruit jam or preserves you like in these cookies; or for a chocolate fix, try a chocolate kiss or mini peanut butter cup.

TO REFRIGERATE: You can keep the uncooked, unformed dough refrigerated for up to three days. To cook, follow the instructions above.

TO FREEZE: The formed and filled but uncooked cookies can be frozen on their baking sheets. Transfer the frozen cookies to a large, resealable plastic bag in the freezer for up to three months. To serve, remove as many of the cookies as you need, and bake according to the instructions above, adding 2 or 3 minutes to the baking time.

VEGETARIAN

SLICE-AND-BAKE LEMON COOKIES

MAKES ABOUT 18 COOKIES • PREP TIME: 10 MINUTES, PLUS 1 HOUR TO CHILL DOUGH • COOK TIME: 15 MINUTES

Keep a log of this cookie dough in the freezer, and you can make fresh-baked cookies any day on demand. This dough is also ideal for rolling out and cutting into decorative shapes, and for frosting and sprinkling with colorful decorations.

1½ cups all-purpose flour

¼ teaspoon fine sea salt

½ cup (1 stick) unsalted butter, at room temperature

½ cup sugar

1 large egg

½ teaspoon vanilla extract

Finely grated zest of 1 lemon

In a medium mixing bowl, whisk the flour and salt together.

In a large bowl, or in the bowl of a stand mixer, cream together the butter and sugar until light and fluffy, 3 to 5 minutes. Add the egg, vanilla, and lemon zest, and mix to incorporate.

With the mixer running on low speed, add the flour mixture slowly to the butter mixture. Beat gently until well combined.

Place the dough onto a sheet of parchment paper. Using your hands, dusted with a bit of flour to prevent sticking, form the dough into a log about 2 inches in diameter. Wrap the dough log tightly in the parchment paper. To store the cookies for baking later, skip ahead to the storage instructions. If you plan to bake them straight away, chill the log for at least 1 hour.

To bake, preheat the oven to 325°F.

Cover a large baking sheet with parchment paper. Using a sharp knife, slice the dough log into ¼-inch-thick slices, and arrange them on the prepared baking sheet. Bake for about 13 minutes, until the edges begin to turn golden brown. Transfer to a wire rack to cool.

TIP: For an extra touch of citrus, top the cookies with a quick lemon glaze after they've cooled completely. To make the glaze, combine ¼ cup freshly squeezed lemon juice with ½ cup powdered sugar and 1 teaspoon melted butter. Whisk until smooth and drizzle over the cooled cookies.

TO REFRIGERATE: The dough log can be kept in the refrigerator for up to three days. To bake the cookies, follow the instructions above.

TO FREEZE: Place the parchment-wrapped dough log into a large, resealable plastic bag, and store in the freezer for up to three months. To bake the cookies, let the dough log thaw for a few minutes, then slice and bake as many cookies as desired following the instructions above. Rewrap and refreeze the remainder of the dough log.

VEGETARIAN

CHOCOLATE-GINGER COOKIES

MAKES ABOUT 4 DOZEN COOKIES • PREP TIME: 15 MINUTES • COOK TIME: 20 MINUTES

These cookies bring together two very different but equally beloved flavors, with the spicy ginger playing beautifully against a subtle background of earthy dark chocolate. I find these cookies equally satisfying dunked into a hot cup of coffee or a cold glass of milk.

¾ cup plus 2 tablespoons sugar, divided
¼ cup melted coconut oil
2 tablespoons plus 2 teaspoons molasses
1 large egg white
1½ cups almond flour
1¾ teaspoons baking soda
2 tablespoons unsweetened cocoa powder
2 teaspoons ground ginger
2 teaspoons cinnamon
½ teaspoon fine sea salt

Preheat the oven to 350°F (if planning to bake right away).

Line two large baking sheets with parchment paper.

In a large bowl, or in the bowl of a stand mixer, beat together ¾ cup of sugar, the coconut oil, the molasses, and the egg white. Add the almond flour, baking soda, cocoa powder, ginger, cinnamon, and salt, and beat on medium speed until incorporated.

Spread the remaining 2 tablespoons of sugar in a shallow dish. Form the cookie dough into 1½-inch balls, then roll each ball in the sugar to coat.

Arrange the balls on the prepared baking sheet and flatten them to about ½ inch thick with your hand or the back of a spoon. To freeze, skip ahead to the storage instructions below.

Bake the cookies in the preheated oven for about 17 minutes, just until they begin to brown around the edges. Remove the baking sheet from the oven and let the cookies cool on the pan for 5 minutes before transferring them to a wire rack to cool completely.

TO STORE: The baked cookies will keep in an airtight container at room temperature for up to a week.

TO FREEZE: Freeze the formed but unbaked cookies on their baking sheet until frozen solid, at least 2 hours. Then transfer to a large, resealable plastic bag and keep frozen for up to three months. To cook, preheat the oven to 350°F, line a baking sheet with parchment paper, arrange the number of cookies (still frozen) you want to bake on the sheet, and bake for about 20 minutes, just until they begin to brown around the edges.

GLUTEN-FREE

DAIRY-FREE

OATMEAL RAISIN COOKIES

I make sure to have a bag of formed but unbaked cookies in the freezer at all times. That way, whenever a craving strikes, I can bake as many as I need. These oatmeal cookies freeze especially well, and you can't beat them fresh out of the oven once they've been baked.

1½ cups whole-wheat flour

1 teaspoon baking soda

1 teaspoon baking powder

½ teaspoon fine sea salt

1 teaspoon cinnamon

¾ cup coconut oil

1 cup (packed) light brown sugar

2 large eggs

1 tablespoon vanilla extract

2 ¾ cups instant oats or old-fashioned rolled oats

1 ¼ cups raisins

Preheat the oven to 375°F.

Line a large baking sheet with parchment paper.

In a medium mixing bowl, stir together the flour, baking soda, baking powder, salt, and cinnamon.

In a separate large mixing bowl, combine the coconut oil, sugar, eggs, and vanilla, and mix well.

Add the flour mixture to the wet ingredients, and stir to mix. Add the oats and raisins, and stir gently to incorporate them.

Scoop the dough onto the prepared baking sheet in heaping tablespoons. Leave at least an inch between the cookies. To freeze or refrigerate, skip ahead to the storage instructions below.

Bake for 13 to 17 minutes, until the cookies are nicely browned. Remove the baking sheet from the oven and let the cookies cool completely before transferring them to a plate or storage container.

GLUTEN-FREE: Use gluten-free oats.

TIP: You can dress up these cookies with whatever add-ins you like. Try adding chopped walnuts or chocolate chips, or swapping dried cherries or blueberries for the raisins.

TO REFRIGERATE: The unbaked cookie dough can be stored in the refrigerator for up to three days. To bake, follow the instructions above.

TO FREEZE: Transfer the baking sheet with the formed but unbaked cookies to the freezer. Freeze until frozen solid, at least 2 hours. Transfer the cookies to a large, resealable plastic bag. To bake, preheat the oven to 375°F and bake from frozen on a parchment-lined baking sheet for 15 to 18 minutes.

VEGETARIAN

DAIRY-FREE

SUPER MOIST GLUTEN-FREE CARROT CAKE

SERVES 8 • PREP TIME: 10 MINUTES • COOK TIME: 40 MINUTES

Almond flour replaces wheat flour in this recipe, giving the cake a dense texture without making it dry. This cake's extraordinary moistness is accentuated by eggs, lots of grated carrot, and a bit of yogurt. If you prefer, you can also make this cake in the form of muffins, reducing the cooking time to about 25 minutes.

3 tablespoons cooking oil, plus additional for preparing the pan

2 large eggs

¼ cup plain yogurt

1 teaspoon vanilla extract

2 cups almond flour

1 cup sugar

2 teaspoons baking powder

1 teaspoon pumpkin pie spice

¼ teaspoon fine sea salt

2 large carrots, finely grated

Preheat the oven to 350°F.

Lightly oil an 8-by-8-inch square cake pan. If you plan to freeze the cake whole, line the pan with foil, with enough overhang that you'll be able to use it to lift the cake out of the pan.

In a large mixing bowl or the bowl of a stand mixer, beat together the eggs, yogurt, vanilla, and 3 tablespoons of oil.

In a separate bowl, whisk together the almond flour, sugar, baking powder, pumpkin pie spice, and salt. Add the dry mixture to the egg mixture, and mix well. Stir in the carrots.

Pour the batter into the prepared cake pan and bake in the preheated oven for about 40 minutes, until a toothpick inserted in the center comes out clean. Set the pan on a wire rack to cool completely.

DAIRY-FREE: Use nondairy yogurt.

TIP: To make a quick cream-cheese frosting to top the cake, beat together 4 ounces of cream cheese, ¾ to 1 cup powdered sugar, and ½ teaspoon vanilla.

TO REFRIGERATE: The cake will keep in the refrigerator, covered with plastic wrap, for up to a week.

TO FREEZE: You can freeze the cake whole by covering the pan tightly with plastic wrap. If you've lined the pan with foil, lift the cake out carefully and wrap it tightly with plastic wrap. You can also slice the cake into serving-size pieces and freeze them on a baking sheet. Once the slices are frozen, wrap them tightly in plastic wrap and transfer to a large, resealable plastic bag. To serve, unwrap the cake or cake slices, and thaw in the refrigerator overnight.

VEGETARIAN

GLUTEN-FREE

179

DESSERTS

FLOURLESS ORANGE CAKE

This simple cake is based on a traditional Sicilian recipe. It uses almond flour instead of wheat, cutting down on carbohydrates while providing protein and other essential nutrients. This unpretentious cake may consist of just six ingredients, but the taste is truly special.

2 large oranges, plus 1 tablespoon zest
3 large eggs
¾ cup sugar
3 cups almond flour
½ teaspoon vanilla extract
1 teaspoon baking powder

Preheat the oven to 350°F.

Set aside the orange zest.

Peel both oranges and remove any seeds. Place the fruit in a food processor, and purée until smooth. Measure out 1 cup of this purée and discard the rest.

In a large bowl, beat the eggs with the sugar until light and creamy. Add the orange purée, along with the zest, and beat to incorporate. Add the almond flour, vanilla, and baking powder, and beat to combine.

Transfer the batter to a 9-inch springform pan or a loaf pan. Bake in the preheated oven for about 55 minutes, until the top is golden brown and a toothpick inserted into the center of the cake comes out clean.

Transfer the pan to a wire rack and cool for 10 minutes. Remove the cake from the pan and let cool completely on the wire rack.

TIP: When ready to serve, dust the top with powdered sugar, or make a glaze of powdered sugar and orange juice to drizzle over the top.

TO REFRIGERATE: Wrap the cake tightly in plastic wrap and store in the refrigerator for up to a week. To serve, bring to room temperature.

TO FREEZE: Wrap the whole cake tightly in plastic wrap, or slice the cake into wedges and wrap each wedge in plastic wrap. Freeze for up to three months. To serve, thaw in the refrigerator overnight or at room temperature for several hours. Bring to room temperature before serving.

VEGETARIAN

GLUTEN-FREE

DAIRY-FREE

FLOURLESS CHOCOLATE FUDGE BROWNIES

MAKES 9 BROWNIES • PREP TIME: 10 MINUTES • COOK TIME: 30 MINUTES

These fudgy brownies are so chocolaty, you'd never guess they're made with black beans. But it's actually the beans that make them so moist. Feel free to add chopped nuts or chocolate chips to the batter before baking.

3 tablespoons melted unsalted butter, plus additional for preparing the pan

1 (15-ounce) can black beans, rinsed and drained

2 large eggs

¾ cup unsweetened cocoa powder

¼ teaspoon fine sea salt

1 teaspoon vanilla extract

½ cup plus 2 tablespoons sugar

Preheat the oven to 350°F.

Lightly butter a 9-by-9-inch square baking pan.

In a food processor, combine the butter, beans, eggs, cocoa powder, salt, vanilla, and sugar, and process until very smooth, scraping down the sides of the bowl as needed.

Transfer the batter to the prepared baking pan and bake in the preheated oven for 25 to 30 minutes, until the top is dry and you can see the edges pulling away from the sides of the pan.

Let cool in the pan for about 30 minutes before cutting.

DAIRY-FREE: Use melted coconut oil instead of butter.

TIP: You can also make these in a standard 12-cup muffin tin for perfectly round, single-serving brownies. Just reduce the cooking time by 5 minutes.

TO REFRIGERATE: Wrap tightly in plastic wrap and store in the refrigerator for up to a week.

TO FREEZE: Wrap the brownies individually in plastic wrap and put them in a large, resealable plastic bag. Freeze for up to three months. To serve, thaw in the refrigerator overnight or at room temperature for several hours.

VEGETARIAN

GLUTEN-FREE

CHOCOLATE-COVERED COCONUT TRUFFLES

MAKES ABOUT 18 TRUFFLES • PREP TIME: 15 MINUTES, PLUS 1 HOUR
TO CHILL • COOK TIME: NONE

These chocolate-coated treats filled with creamy coconut are made with surprisingly healthy ingredients. Unsweetened coconut is mixed with coconut oil, which hardens when chilled and holds the mixture together. The chocolate shell is a sweet bonus.

2 cups shredded, unsweetened coconut
¼ cup honey
¼ cup plus 1 tablespoon coconut oil
1 teaspoon vanilla extract
4 ounces milk or semisweet chocolate chips

In a food processor, pulse the coconut until it has the consistency of flour.

In a medium bowl, combine the processed coconut, honey, coconut oil, and vanilla, and stir to mix well.

Form the mixture into about eighteen 1½-inch balls, arranging them on a baking sheet or platter as they're formed. Transfer the baking sheet to the freezer and chill until firm, about 30 minutes. To speed up the chilling, you could put them in the freezer for 15 minutes.

Put the chocolate chips in a small, microwave-safe bowl, and heat at 50 percent power in 30-second intervals, stirring after each interval, until completely melted and smooth.

Cover a baking sheet with parchment paper. Dip the chilled coconut balls in the melted chocolate one at a time, using two forks to roll them around to make sure they are fully covered. Remove them from the bowl, letting the excess chocolate drip back into the bowl. Arrange the coated balls on the baking sheet. Refrigerate or freeze until the chocolate has hardened.

DAIRY-FREE: Use vegan chocolate.

VEGAN: Substitute maple syrup for the honey and use vegan chocolate.

TIP: To make these healthy little candies taste like Almond Joy bars, form each coconut ball around a whole almond, and use milk chocolate for the coating.

TO REFRIGERATE: The truffles can be stored, covered, in the refrigerator for up to a week. Serve chilled.

TO FREEZE: Freeze the truffles on the baking sheet until frozen solid, at least two hours. Transfer to a large, resealable plastic bag and keep in the freezer for up to three months. To serve, thaw in the refrigerator for several hours.

VEGETARIAN

GLUTEN-FREE

SUPERFOOD CHOCOLATE BARK

MAKES ABOUT 1 ¾ POUNDS • PREP TIME: 10 MINUTES,
PLUS 30 MINUTES TO CHILL • COOK TIME: NONE

Dark chocolate is known as a "superfood" because it's full of antioxidants that help protect against disease. This easy-to-make treat turns a sweet indulgence into a veritable health food by topping dark chocolate with other superfoods like almonds, tart cherries, and coconut.

1½ pounds dark chocolate, chopped, divided
¾ teaspoon vanilla extract
¼ cup plus 2 tablespoons sliced almonds
¼ cup plus 2 tablespoons chopped dried tart cherries
3 tablespoons unsweetened shredded coconut

Line a large, rimmed baking sheet with parchment paper.

Heat 1 pound of chocolate in a double boiler set over a pot of simmering water, stirring continuously, until melted.

Remove the bowl or pan containing the melted chocolate from the heat, and stir in the remaining ½ pound of chocolate until melted. Stir in the vanilla.

Pour the melted chocolate onto the prepared baking sheet, spreading it into a smooth, even layer with a rubber spatula. Quickly sprinkle the almonds, cherries, and coconut evenly over the top, and press them down lightly with your fingertips.

Refrigerate or freeze until the chocolate has set, about 30 minutes in the refrigerator or 15 minutes in the freezer. Break the chocolate up into 2- to 3-inch pieces. Keep refrigerated and serve chilled.

PALEO: Substitute vanilla paste for the vanilla extract.

VEGAN: Use vegan dark chocolate.

TIP: You can vary this recipe however you like. Try topping it with walnuts, sunflower seeds, dried blueberries, cranberries, goji berries, or even a healthy breakfast cereal.

TO REFRIGERATE: The chocolate bark can be kept in an airtight container in the refrigerator for up to two weeks.

TO FREEZE: Freeze the chocolate bark for up to six months. Serve directly from the freezer, or thaw in the refrigerator for several hours before serving.

VEGETARIAN

GLUTEN-FREE

DAIRY-FREE

CONVERSION TABLES

VOLUME EQUIVALENTS (LIQUID)

US STANDARD	US STANDARD (OUNCES)	METRIC (APPROXIMATE)
2 tablespoons	1 fl. oz.	30 mL
¼ cup	2 fl. oz.	60 mL
½ cup	4 fl. oz.	120 mL
1 cup	8 fl. oz.	240 mL
1½ cups	12 fl. oz.	355 mL
2 cups or 1 pint	16 fl. oz.	475 mL
4 cups or 1 quart	32 fl. oz.	1 L
1 gallon	128 fl. oz.	4 L

OVEN TEMPERATURES

FAHRENHEIT (F)	CELSIUS (C) (APPROXIMATE)
250°	120°
300°	150°
325°	165°
350°	180°
375°	190°
400°	200°
425°	220°
450°	230°

VOLUME EQUIVALENTS (DRY)

US STANDARD	METRIC (APPROXIMATE)
⅛ teaspoon	0.5 mL
¼ teaspoon	1 mL
½ teaspoon	2 mL
¾ teaspoon	4 mL
1 teaspoon	5 mL
1 tablespoon	15 mL
¼ cup	59 mL
⅓ cup	79 mL
½ cup	118 mL
⅔ cup	156 mL
¾ cup	177 mL
1 cup	235 mL
2 cups or 1 pint	475 mL
3 cups	700 mL
4 cups or 1 quart	1 L

WEIGHT EQUIVALENTS

US STANDARD	METRIC (APPROXIMATE)
½ ounce	15 g
1 ounce	30 g
2 ounces	60 g
4 ounces	115 g
8 ounces	225 g
12 ounces	340 g
16 ounces or 1 pound	455 g

RECIPE INDEX

INDEX

ACKNOWLEDGMENTS

AS ALWAYS, I AM GRATEFUL to my husband, Doug Reil, and my son, Cashel Reil, for their endless support, encouragement, and willingness to try my kitchen experiments. I am also grateful to the team at Callisto Media, including but not limited to my editor, Nana K. Twumasi.

ABOUT THE AUTHOR

ROBIN DONOVAN is a food writer, recipe developer, and author of numerous cookbooks, including the bestselling *Campfire Cuisine* and *Dutch Oven Obsession*. She lives in Berkeley and blogs about super easy recipes for surprisingly delicious meals at www.TwoLazyGourmets.com.